DATING ESSENTIALS FOR MEN

DATING ESSENTIALS FOR MEN

THE ONLY DATING GUIDE YOU WILL EVER NEED

DR. ROBERT GLOVER

PROFESSIONAL DISCLAIMER

Although you may find the information, principles, applications, and assignments in this book to be useful, they are presented with the understanding that the author is not engaged in providing specific medical, psychological, emotional, or sexual advice. Nor is anything in this book intended to be a diagnosis, prescription, recommendation, or cure for any specific kind of medical, psychological, emotional, or sexual problem.

Each person has unique needs, and this book cannot take these individual differences into account. Each person should engage in a program of treatment, prevention, cure, and/or general health only in consultation with licensed, qualified physicians, therapists, and/or other competent professionals.

DEDICATION

Dating Essentials for Men is dedicated to every man who is willing to step out of his comfort zone, challenge his distorted and self-limiting beliefs, and practice effective dating and relational skills. May these men find all the love and sex they desire.

TABLE OF CONTENTS

Introduction: Dating Essentials for Men xiii

Part 1: Mastering Your Mind. 1
Chapter 1: Blast the Lies Your Mind Tells You About
    Yourself and Women 3
Chapter 2: The Joy of Dating – Uncover and Overcome
    Your Self-Limiting Beliefs 12
Chapter 3: Eliminate Your Fear of Rejection – Forever! 20
Chapter 4: Discover the Power of Abundance Thinking. 26
Chapter 5: Overcome Your Anxiety with Women 36
Chapter 6: Take a Breath and Soothe Yourself 45
Chapter 7: Use the Secret Women Don't Want You to
    Know to Your Advantage. 51
Chapter 8: Break Your Addiction to Superficial Beauty. 60
Chapter 9: Create a Lifestyle That Attracts Women Naturally. 68
Chapter 10: Activate Women's Basic Biological Urges 80

Part 2: Perfecting Your Practice. 91
Chapter 11: Pay Attention to Detail (She Does). 93
Chapter 12: Use the Internet to Your Advantage 103
Chapter 13: Commit to Going Out with 12 Women in 12 Weeks 115
Chapter 14: Avoid the Number One Mistake Most Men
    Make with Women 127
Chapter 15: Learn and Practice the Secrets of Natural Players. 135
Chapter 16: You've Got Her Attention, Now Drive Up
    Her Interest 144

Chapter 17: Banter and Flirt Like a Pro (Even if You're
    Shy or Introverted) 153
Chapter 18: Follow This Roadmap to Find Your Really
    Great Woman 165
Chapter 19: Practice the Most Important Dating Skill of
    All – Be a Good Ender 174

Dating Essentials for Men Wrap-Up...........................181
Dr. Robert Glover..183
More Dating Essentials for Men Resources 185
Please Leave a Review and Spread the Word 187

INTRODUCTION: DATING ESSENTIALS FOR MEN

This is easy. I can do this!

Are you a bad dater? If so, welcome to the club. So was I and so are most of the men walking the planet. Dating and courting are not in our human DNA. They have only existed in Western culture for a few generations. In the East – not even there yet. For most of modern civilization, marriages were arranged by families and clans. The idea of romantic love has only been around a couple of hundred years. Nevertheless, we live in a world where dating skills are essential for finding companionship, love, a mate, and of course, sexual partners.

I find that many men struggle with the most basic aspects of dating and mating. For most of us, these skills don't come naturally. And, we've never had someone show us the way. The fear of doing something wrong, looking foolish, and getting rejected permeates the minds of most men – regardless of age, physical appearance, and socioeconomic status. This fear typically manifests in clumsy attempts at approach and/or doing nothing at all. The all too common outcome of repeated failure at finding a suitable partner leaves many men feeling defective and unlovable.

I've been there. For the majority of my life, I was a loser with the ladies. And, I assumed the good women I was interested in just weren't interested in me. But that all changed. Let me tell you about it.

When I became single in my mid-forties after 25 years of marriage, I came face to face with the reality that I hadn't dated since college – and that I wasn't good at it even then. Back in high school and college, when I wanted to ask a woman out, I would first spend several weeks imagining what it would be like to be with her. My fear, self-limiting beliefs, and lack of skills prevented me from simply approaching her and asking her out.

When I finally got up the nerve to approach a woman I'd been obsessing about, I would wait until the last minute, walk up to her awkwardly, and blurt out something like, "I don't guess you would want to go out with me tonight, would you?" She would usually respond with a look of surprise and say something like, "Oh, I already have plans." Then, I would feel foolish, retreat, and never talk to her again.

When I did succeed at getting a girlfriend, I would hang onto her forever because I didn't want to repeat the process of having to start dating all over again (I stayed married to two women for a total of 25 years when I shouldn't have gone out on more than three dates with either of them.)

This time around, in my forties, I realized I would have to learn to do things a lot differently. Here's what I did: I began reading and listening to dating and seduction books and CDs, while drawing from insights I wrote about in my book, **No More Mr. Nice Guy**. Then, most importantly, I began applying those principles to see what worked and what didn't. I approached dating as if it were a scientific experiment.

To my surprise, I found that getting a woman to talk to me, give me her phone number, date me, and have sex with me was nowhere nearly as difficult as I thought it would be. In fact, I was frequently amazed at how simple and easy it was when I applied the right principles. Several of my clients noticed that I was having success meeting women (and having a lot of sex) and begged me to teach them what I was doing. Out of these requests, *Dating Essentials for Men* was born.

In 2007, I launched four, four-week online *Dating Essentials for Men* courses. These courses were a compilation of what I had learned through trial and error and a lot of fucking practice. The courses became an instant success because they offered a breath of fresh air from programs that teach men to be cocky/funny, spin plates, or use canned pickup routines. This book is an update and expansion of those four courses.

If you had asked me any time before the age of 45 if I would be teaching men how to date, I would have said you were crazy. But, you know what? If a bad dater like me can learn how to interact confidently with women – get their phone numbers, get laid, and create great relationships – so can you!

In my quest to become an effective dater I discovered many principles that work and many that don't. Much of what I teach in *Dating Essentials for Men* is counterintuitive to what you believe to be true about women, dating, and sex. That's the beauty of the *Dating Essentials for Men* approach.

Most men make dating way too difficult. One of the most common reactions men have to what I present is, "This is easy. I can do this!" *Dating Essentials for Men* makes dating doable – the way it should be.

The principles and practices that I share will challenge you in ways you have never been challenged before. But, showing you how simple it is to talk to women, get their phone numbers, date them, and get them into bed increases the likelihood that you will actually get out there and do it.

Rest assured, I will not turn you into a *geek with techniques* – i.e., a man who has memorized 32 canned openers for working sets, building rapport, or getting a number close – yet who's still terrified of women and lacks basic social skills.

The principles I teach and the tools I share in *Dating Essentials for Men* have helped transform countless bad daters into dating pros. All of these men were guys just like you and me, most with a history of repeated failure in dating. Not to mention insecurities and self-limiting beliefs.

Dating may not be part of our human DNA, but when you know what you're doing and what works, it's surprisingly easy.

What to Expect from *Dating Essentials for Men*

I have found that most guys who purchase my *Dating Essentials for Men* products (classes, workshops, podcasts, etc.) fall into one of two categories:

- Men who have never dated well, had few real girlfriends, and have little or no sex; or
- Men who have recently gotten out of a long-term relationship and are back out in the dating world for the first time in several years.

Occasionally, men sign up for my programs because they have been relatively successful meeting women, but they want to improve their skills and attitudes. Regardless of which category you fall into, the principles I teach will work for you.

Whether you want to learn and practice basic dating skills, develop confidence, have more and better sex, or meet the woman of your dreams, *Dating Essentials for Men* will get you moving in the right direction – and bring you proven results!

Dating Essentials for Men will help you:

- Clearly identify your goals for dating – and achieve them.
- Face your fears and soothe your anxiety.
- Learn new, effective skills for dating, mating, and breaking up.
- Challenge yourself to act and practice new skills.

Dating Essentials for Men focuses on two core areas of dating:

Mastering Your Mind (MYM): The *MYM* parts of *DEFM* will help you become aware of – and challenge – the self-limiting beliefs that keep you stuck at home by yourself every weekend.

Perfecting Your Practice (PYP): The *PYP* parts of *DEFM* will teach you new skills and daily routines to help you meet women and get what you want in love and sex.

Dating Essentials for Men will go after every distorted belief you have about yourself and dating, while challenging you to get out of your comfort zone and discover how easy it is to meet and date lots of great women.

It doesn't matter if you want to date for practice, find a friend with benefits, or meet your Really Great Woman, *Dating Essentials for Men* will teach you how.

Making Miracles

I want to challenge you to bring your *A-game* to this material. Simply purchasing it and leaving it on your computer or tablet won't change a goddamn thing in your life.

There is no substitute for putting the principles of *Dating Essentials for Men* into practice. Don't try to figure out how to do it *right.* Just get out there and do something. And then get out there and do it some more.

It works if you work it.

Relationships usually result from unexpected miracles, and miracles usually happen around *people!*

Not many miracles happen when you're sitting at home playing Xbox, watching television, or surfing the internet for porn. Nor do many miracles happen when you're spending 60 – 70 hours a week at work.

You have to get out of the house and apply the principles presented in *Dating Essentials for Men* to make your miracles happen.

Doing this will be scary, but the moment you face your monster, you will be transformed.

Here is what I constantly tell men:

- Get out of the house.
- Expand your route.
- Linger in public.
- Talk to people everywhere you go.
- Test for interest.
- Walk through open doors.

In reality, *Dating Essentials for Men is about expanding your social and emotional intelligence* – I just use men's desire to get laid and find love as the motivation for helping them grow up and become interesting people.

As you practice the skills I teach in *Dating Essentials for Men*, you will also be working on the following essential life skills:

- Becoming aware of and confronting self-limiting beliefs.
- Stretching yourself and getting out of your comfort zone.
- Letting go of attachment to outcome.
- Setting the tone and taking the lead.
- Getting to rejection quickly.
- Becoming a *good ender.*

Not only will *DEFM* help you get the love and sex you want, it will help you become a more complete, confident person.

Here's a little secret: When I transformed my love life using the skills I teach in *Dating Essentials for Men*, I also transformed every other part of my life:

- My income increased.
- Many unexpected adventures came my way.
- My business grew.
- I made new friends.
- My overall satisfaction in life skyrocketed.

Are you ready to join the thousands of men who have successfully transformed their dating and love lives? If so, make the investment in yourself.

I guarantee you'll love the new you!

Dr. Robert Glover

PART 1: MASTERING YOUR MIND

Most men's dating struggles have very little to do with the reasons they think. I've heard all the excuses:

- I'm too short.
- I'm not experienced enough.
- I'm boring.
- Women can see right through me.
- All women are gold-diggers and they only want tall guys with money.
- I come too quickly.
- I can't get or stay hard.
- I have a small dick.
- I have social anxiety.
- I'm introverted.
- I don't know where to start.
- I'm afraid of looking foolish.
- I'm afraid of getting beat up.
- The women I'm interested in aren't interested in me.
- All the good women are in a relationship.
- Blah, blah, blah.
- Wah, wah, wah.

As I said, I've heard them all (and even believed a few myself).

No matter how strongly you believe these excuses to be true, and no matter how much evidence you can dredge up to support your beliefs, they are lies. They are lies your mind tells you, and they are lies you're happy to believe. Why? Because they let you off the hook.

Here's the deal: To successfully date, get laid, and have great relationships, you have to challenge yourself. You have to be willing to face your fears and leave your comfort zone.

All of the above excuses keep you safe. They keep you in the nursery where everything is warm and cozy.

Dating Essentials for Men will show you the way out of the nursery and into the world of bold masculinity. Practicing what I teach in this book will allow you to grow as a man, and lead you to the love and sex that you want.

We will begin with the problem between your ears – your *self-limiting beliefs* (SLBs as I call them). These false beliefs prevent you from getting what you want in all areas of life.

The *MYM* section of *Dating Essentials for Men* won't just challenge the validity of all your SLBs – it will completely blow them out of the water.

Ready? Let's dive in.

CHAPTER 1: BLAST THE LIES YOUR MIND TELLS YOU ABOUT YOURSELF AND WOMEN

The world we have created is a product of our thinking. It cannot change without changing our thinking. – Albert Einstein

Believe it or not, your mind lies to you all the time. The genius, Albert Einstein, understood this. The biggest lies your mind tells you are usually about yourself and women. This chapter is going to help you identify these lies, understand their effect on you, and blast them away so you can start getting what you want in love, sex, and relationships.

Sound good?

Bad Daters

Most bad daters (BDs) struggle with three fundamental problems:

Isolation

Bad daters tend to avoid social situations in which they might have to talk to people they don't know. BDs often suffer from some degree of social anxiety, which is especially pronounced around desirable women. To reduce their anxiety, BDs keep to themselves and take few social risks.

Lack of Skills

Most bad daters have never acquired the fundamental skills of dating, mating, and breaking up. This is understandable. In many cultures, there is no custom of dating. Even in western society where there is some history of courtship, it has only existed for a half-century or so. The whole idea of romantic love has only existed for a couple of hundred years.

If you lack basic dating skills, you are not alone. Most men have never learned how to banter, flirt, test, close the deal, or break up with a woman. This often results in a general lack of confidence. Consequently, BDs tend to avoid women or become friends with women they desire, hoping this will eventually lead to deeper intimacy.

Self-Limiting Beliefs

Most bad daters struggle with issues of self-acceptance and confidence. This lack of self-esteem is the result of their SLBs. Bad daters tend to be riddled with these beliefs. They typically believe that women can tell they are losers just by looking at them. They are consumed with negative self-messages:

- I'm too fat.
- I'm inexperienced.
- I can't handle rejection.
- Why would a good woman want me?
- I don't have much sexual experience.
- I'm boring.
- All the good women are taken.

For bad daters, SLBs become self-perpetuating realities that keep them stuck and frustrated. The chapters in the *MYM* section of *Dating Essentials for Men* will focus on uncovering and overcoming your SLBs about yourself, women, and the world in general. These chapters will probably cause tremendous inner turmoil for you because they will challenge everything you believe to be true. *Your mind has been telling you unsubstantiated lies about yourself, women, and the world for most of your life. We are going to challenge these lies.*

This will make you anxious because *your mind believes what your mind tells you to be true.* Your mind has been lying to you for years, but you've had no reason to be suspicious of this insidious inner deceit.

As we uncover these lies and shine the bright light of reality on them, your mind will go into overdrive to hang onto what it believes to be true.

As you experience this inner mental struggle, your mind will try and convince you to keep believing the lies it's been feeding you. This is normal.

Just remember: Historically, *your best thinking has gotten you exactly where you are right now* – lonely and frustrated. When it comes to how you view yourself, women, and dating, we are going to be suspicious of everything your mind has believed to be true.

As you do the work in this course, your brain will frequently shout things like:

- BULLSHIT!
- That's not true!
- I can't do that!
- Women aren't like that!
- If I did that, I'd get slapped!
- That might work for other guys, but it won't for me!

Whenever you hear these excuses in your head, pay attention to them and state them out loud (yes, actually say them out loud).

This chapter will help you identify, explore, and overcome the lies that prevent you from approaching women, asking for their phone numbers, taking them out, getting them into bed, and creating long-term, loving relationships. The following chapters will build on this process. This information will blast the SLBs out of your mind and help you start getting what you want in love, sex, and relationships.

"What gets us into trouble is not what we don't know. It's what we know for sure that just ain't so." – Mark Twain

Toxic Shame

In *No More Mr. Nice Guy*, I discuss the effects of *toxic shame* as it relates to the Nice Guy Syndrome. Toxic shame is the deeply held, unconscious belief that you are bad, defective, or unlovable. It is the result of the inaccurate internalization of life events from birth on.

When you experienced neglect, abandonment, inconsistent nurturing, smothering, or emotional, verbal, or physical abuse as a child, you inaccurately internalized that you were the cause. You believed there must be something wrong with you that caused the painful things you were experiencing.

What makes these early life experiences so debilitating is that the events and the interpretation of the events were stored up in a part of your brain that has no language or reasoning capability. The first part of your brain that developed as a child is called the *Amygdala*. It is often referred to as the *primal brain*. It is the source of the *fight-flight-freeze* mechanism. Again, this emotional storehouse of your mind does not have language or reasoning capability. It operates on a purely primal survival basis.

The *cortex* is the reasoning and language part of your brain that developed later and more slowly. It got going at age four or five and didn't fully develop until you were around age 25. That is why young men's auto insurance rates are so high. The part of the brain responsible for making good decisions isn't fully developed in men until their mid-twenties.

This means that everything that happened to you in the first few years of your life was stored up in the emotional part of your brain, not the reasoning part. The internalization of early life events, along with heredity (your inherited temperament goes a long way in determining how you interpret your early life experiences), determines your emotional personality.

The thinking part of your brain unquestioningly accepts everything recorded in the emotional centers of your brain to be one hundred percent accurate.

These emotional beliefs are your mental operating system. They are your *machine language* or the *DOS* of your brain.

Your thinking and reasoning rises out of and reflects your unconscious emotional paradigm. *Your mind will always work to make sure your mental beliefs are consistent with the non-verbal, emotional beliefs you internalized as a young child.*

Even though toxic shame is a purely emotional experience, you attach words and thoughts to this deep, uncomfortable feeling. You might say you feel lonely, isolated, anxious, fearful, bad or unloved. You then attach personal meaning to these feelings.

"I feel depressed because no one likes me."

"I'm lonely because I'm not good enough."

"When people find out how defective I really am, they all leave me."

"If I were taller, thinner, smarter, more outgoing, richer, etc., etc., then I wouldn't feel so lonely."

Since every human being grows up in an imperfect family and in an imperfect world, everyone internalizes some degree of toxic shame in childhood. As you grew into adolescence and adulthood, you continued to add evidence from life's events that seemed to support the emotional beliefs you internalized at a young age. This is called the *paradigm effect*.

The Paradigm Effect

Here is how paradigms work: You seek out, amplify, and retain information that seems to support your SLBs. But, any information that seems to contradict or challenge the validity of your SLBs you'll minimize or rationalize away, or simply won't notice.

Here is an example:

If an attractive woman smiles at you or talks to you, you assume that she is just being polite or smiling at someone else because such behavior contradicts your SLBs.

The cycle then repeats itself over and over again.

Your SLBs that come from toxic shame have their greatest impact on your personal relationships. *If you believe that you are defective and unlovable, you will also assume that everyone else sees you the same way.*

Why would you ask a woman out if you are convinced you are defective and she will reject you? Why would you let people know you deeply if they are just going to find out how imperfect you are?

Due to toxic shame, your SLBs convince you that attractive women are not attracted to you:

- Therefore: Because you believe this to be true, you don't interact with women you find attractive.
- Therefore: Because you don't interact with attractive women, they tend not to notice you or interact with you.
- Therefore: You then use this data to reinforce the belief that attractive women aren't interested in you which, of course, means you continue to avoid interacting with them.

How Self-Limiting Beliefs Affect Dating

The self-limiting beliefs attached to your toxic shame are the biggest problem hindering you from getting what you want in love and sex. Here are some of the ways your SLBs affect your dating:

How You Think is How You Are

What you think about and believe to be true is what you will create. Your mindset will determine how you interact with women and how they respond to you.

If you are telling yourself, "I'm a worthless piece of shit," how do you think you will approach women (if at all) and how do you think they will respond to you?

If you are telling yourself, "I'm an interesting, great guy and women really like me," how do you think you will approach women and how do you think they will respond to you?

Your Self-Limiting Beliefs Quietly Encourage You to Isolate and Avoid

Most of the time you aren't aware of your self-limiting beliefs because they whisper in the back of your consciousness:

- Just stay home tonight.
- Don't talk to her, she wouldn't be interested.
- Go ahead and stay on the internet a little longer.
- Don't make eye contact; she'll think you're a pervert!

It isn't until you consciously put yourself into a situation that challenges your SLBs or an unexpected opportunity presents itself, that these voices shout louder in your conscious mind.

"Are you crazy? What the hell do you think you are doing? If you talk to her, she'll just reject you and you'll look like a fool. Look down now. Keep on walking. Whew, that was close. You're such a loser, you'll never have a woman like her. Don't even think about it."

When it is all over, you tell yourself, "See, attractive women never talk to me." It becomes a self-reinforcing cycle.

Your Self-Limiting Beliefs Create Negative Emotions

Not only do SLBs get in the way of you taking action, but they also create negative emotional states. If your mind keeps telling you that you have low self-esteem, that you aren't attractive, or that you're a lousy lover, you will naturally feel bad.

Additionally, because your SLBs prevent you from taking actions that would improve your life, you become even further depressed. Because it feels normal for you to feel bad, and because feeling bad reinforces your SLBs, and because your SLBs make you feel bad, a vicious cycle is perpetuated throughout your life.

Your Self-Limiting Beliefs Cause You to Date Down, Settle, and Stay Too Long in Bad Relationships

Because of your SLBs, you probably date down and settle for women you don't enjoy or who don't turn you on. Your SLBs have probably caused you to stay in bad or unfulfilling relationships way too long because you don't think there are many good women out there. And, even if there are good women out there, you don't believe you could ever get one. You might as well stay right where you are.

Your Self-Limiting Beliefs Prevent You From Seeing and Walking Through Open Doors

Because of your SLBs, you don't walk through open doors or take advantage of opportunities presented to you. (Raise your hand if you've had a chance to date/sleep with a woman you desired but didn't take advantage of the opportunity when it presented itself because of your SLBs).

Your Self-Limiting Beliefs Keep You Safe

Jeremy had been in one of my single men's groups for several months. In his late thirties, he was smart, funny, and athletic. He had a great job and a nice condo. He had only been in two short-term relationships in his life. Even though he came to group regularly, he never put any real effort into actually applying what he was learning.

During a discussion on self-limiting beliefs, I asked Jeremy what he was afraid a woman might find out about him if she really got to know him. He listed two or three things that he was certain would cause any woman to reject him. I asked him how he knew this to be true. His response was that the two women he had dated had both broken up with him. He took that as proof that all women would find him defective and leave him.

Jeremy's SLBs were obviously there to keep him safe. If he didn't take a risk, he wouldn't get hurt. When I challenged the validity of his beliefs, he hung on tightly to the fact that since he was "batting a thousand" in the rejection department, there must be something wrong with him. His mind completely tuned out any possibility that these women might have been insecure or dysfunctional themselves and that an *N of 2* wouldn't stand up in any research study (he had a science background). Nevertheless, Jeremy continued to hang on tightly to beliefs that kept him feeling safe.

Challenge Your Beliefs

A belief is a thought you keep thinking. Your mind thinks your beliefs are true because you have always thought them. Because your mind strives for consistency, it finds plenty of evidence to support your beliefs (and ignores information that is contradictory). Many of your beliefs about yourself, women, and sex aren't necessarily true or accurate, but your mind believes them because it has repeatedly thought them.

For example, a client of mine lamented that he had given up hope of finding his *Really Great Woman* (RGW). He told me that he didn't find many women all that interesting. The few women he did find to be interesting were married or in a relationship. He stated that he had given up ever finding the kind of woman he would really want to get involved with. How do you think this belief system was playing out in his life?

I suggested to my client that what he believed to be true, would become true. As long as his mind kept telling him that "all the good women are taken," he would be sure he'd never find one. I suggested that he start repeating the following mantra to himself several times a day:

"In the next 30 days, I am going to meet three women who have the potential to be my Really Great Woman. They are available and looking for me."

I told him his job was to put himself in a position to meet these women and walk through the open doors. Doing so included challenging his self-limiting beliefs, getting out of the house, talking to people, working on making himself into the kind of man a great woman would want, and not spending too much time with any women who didn't have the potential to be his RGW.

After just a week or two, my client told me that repeating this mantra made him more optimistic. He had started noticing and interacting with a number of really interesting women. He began approaching women whom he thought might be potential matches because he hated to miss an opportunity. He found that he was in a consistently better mood and taking better care of himself. He ended an on and off again relationship with a woman he had been involved with for a couple of years.

Within three months of repeating this mantra regularly to himself, a mutual friend introduced him to a woman who matched every quality he had been looking for. This woman was intelligent, stable, active, attractive, and available. He reports that he knows he never would have found such a great match if he hadn't worked on changing his negative, deprivation way of thinking. He also realized that even if this relationship didn't work out, it was still proof that great women are out there.

CHAPTER 2: THE JOY OF DATING — UNCOVER AND OVERCOME YOUR SELF-LIMITING BELIEFS

Your mind believes what your mind tells itself is
true, and it is wrong more often than not.

Dating activates your self-limiting beliefs like nothing else. This is good news. SLBs affect every part of your life and keep you stuck and unhappy. By challenging your self-limiting beliefs through the process of dating, you can clear out these mental lies and start experiencing all kinds of great things in life.

Think for a moment what *dating* really is. When you decide you want to date, you are deciding to present yourself to the women of the world and ask them the following question: "In spite of all of my visible flaws (and all the ones you can't see yet, but which I'm painfully aware of), do you find me interesting enough to talk to me, give me your phone number, go out with me, sleep with me, and maybe become my girlfriend?"

If this doesn't bring up every one of your SLBs, I don't know what will! Dating can trigger your inner shame and make you believe you are totally worthless like nothing else can.

I suggest we look at dating in a whole new light. Don't look at dating as an attempt to get women to like you, sleep with you, marry you, etc. *Look at dating as the most effective way imaginable to clean out all the distorted mental crap you've been packing around inside you since birth*. The bonus is that you will also get the love and sex you have been looking for.

Here is what I personally discovered after applying the dating principles I am teaching you in this book: Not only was I going on plenty of dates and having lots of sex, but I was also experiencing amazing success in every other area of my life – work, money, friendship, etc. My business took off. I started making more money than ever before. Personal and social opportunities presented themselves to me right and left. All of these things happened because dating helped me uncover and overcome my latent self-limiting beliefs.

Types of Self-Limiting Beliefs

When it comes to dating, SLBs can take many different forms and occur in many different situations.

There are the self-limiting beliefs that lead to inactivity. Because you don't believe you are attractive or desirable, you pretty much keep to yourself and don't talk to women.

Other SLBs pop up when you are actually presented with an opportunity. "She smiled at me and said hello. Should I talk to her? What should I say? I'll probably just say something stupid. Maybe I misinterpreted her friendliness. What if I make a fool of myself? What if everyone sees? I'm just not good at this. I'll just get my coffee and leave."

Then there are the SLBs that repeat themselves in your mind after a missed opportunity. "Why did I freeze up? I'm such a loser! She seemed to like me, but I never get it right. I'll never have a girlfriend. Why try? I'm worthless."

You can have self-limiting beliefs about every aspect of dating. These include beliefs about you, a particular woman, all women, sex, and the world in general.

- About You: "I'm too …. (fat, poor, shy, etc.)" "I'm not …. (rich, tall, young, etc.) enough." "Attractive women don't talk to me." "I'm a loser."
- About a Particular Woman: "She is so pretty; she probably has a boyfriend." "She would only date a really successful guy."

- About All Women: "Women have all the control." "All women want a successful man." "Women don't like sex." "All the good women are taken."
- About Sex: "I'm a bad man if I want sex." "I don't believe I can satisfy a woman." "Women think men who want sex are bad."
- About the World: "Good things happen to other people, not me." "There is only so much to go around." "It is only a matter of time until the other shoe drops."

Becoming Aware of Self-Limiting Beliefs

In my seminars, I regularly have the guys take turns being the *group SLB secretary*. The secretary's job is to write down the other group members' self-limiting beliefs as they come up. It is amazing how these SLBs just pop out of guys' mouths when they aren't even aware of them. I point them out and request that the secretary write them down. Here are some of the ones that come up frequently:

- A woman will think I'm hitting on her.
- People will think I'm a dirty old man.
- Women will think I'm sleazy.
- Women will think I'm a serial killer.
- I might get rejected.
- I might be intruding.
- I don't deserve a loving relationship.
- I'm not good with small talk.
- I won't have anything interesting to say.
- I might fail.
- I don't want to come on too strong.
- What if she is in a relationship?
- I don't want to be phony or fake.
- I can't see myself doing it.
- I might make a fool of myself.
- I might piss a woman off.
- She'll tell all her friends if I can't get it up.
- I don't want to be a jerk.

- I'll have to give up too much to be in a relationship.
- I don't want women to think I'm a player.
- I have low self-esteem.
- It is easier for other people than it is for me.
- I'm shy.
- I lack confidence.

Do any of these sound familiar?

Emotionally-Laden Language

Another way to become aware of your SLBs is to pay attention to your *emotionally-laden language*. When bad daters talk about their experience with women and dating, they often use strong emotional terms that reveal their self-limiting beliefs. I have to point these words and phrases out to them because they don't usually realize how much negative energy they project onto these situations. This negative energy is just one more manifestation of their SLBs.

Your words are a window to your thoughts:

- She shot me down. vs. She said no.
- I blew it again. vs. It didn't work out.
- I must have done something really wrong. vs. She had a negative reaction.
- Women are all gold-diggers. vs. I'm afraid I won't be able to support a woman.
- I got rejected. vs. She had low interest.

Get Out of Your Comfort Zone

One of the most powerful tools for calling up your SLBs into consciousness is to *do something outside your comfort zone that challenges you.*

- Go places you don't usually go.
- Talk to everyone you meet.
- Make and hold eye contact.
- Ask a woman to meet you for coffee.

- Tell a woman to give you her phone number.

When you do anything that challenges your self-limiting beliefs head on, they will quit whispering at you and start SCREAMING at you! This makes it a lot easier to find out what they are!

For example, I wanted to learn how to salsa dance. I thought it looked cool and it seemed like a great way to meet women. There was only one problem; I had huge negative beliefs about my ability to dance. As a middle-age white guy, my SLBs shouted, "You can't do that, you have no rhythm, you'll look foolish, and people will think you're just cruising for women."

I decided to consciously challenge these voices head on by signing up for a five-week salsa class. My beliefs were so strong that I had to sign up for the class three times before I worked up the courage to go even once. Once I started, I kept going. Nevertheless, my SLBs tried to talk me out of going to class for months. By forcing myself to go to class anyway, I got to hear my negative thought-talk shout at me loud and clear, "You have to do it perfectly, because If you don't, you'll look foolish and people will laugh at you."

These SLBs had always been in my head, whispering in the background. It wasn't until I consciously did something to bring them to the surface that I got to hear them loud and clear. Then, I was able to evaluate whether or not they were accurate. I discovered they were just lies. Cleaning out these self-limiting beliefs through salsa positively affected many other areas of my life.

Even though your emotional makeup and SLBs were pretty well established early in your life, you can use other parts of your mind to overcome your hardwired emotional tendencies. As stated before, this is one of the great things about dating. Dating will call up your self-limiting beliefs like nothing else can.

Why You Started Lying to Yourself

The problems you have experienced getting the love and sex you want is the direct result of a lifetime of believing and acting upon a boatload of false, distorted, negative, and judgmental self-limiting beliefs.

All of your SLBs are the result of repeatedly internalizing inaccurate interpretations of life's events. Your mind has been telling you these things since you were a child and you have found plenty of evidence to support these beliefs through adolescence and adulthood.

For example, your beliefs about yourself and your desirability to women we're probably strongly influenced by your interactions with adolescent girls when you were in middle school. You weren't very mature or socially experienced and neither were the girls. When you started noticing these interesting and unpredictable creatures, you had no idea how to get their attention in a positive way. To you, it seemed these girls had all the power. You believed they could see right through you.

More than likely, you either avoided them or approached them clumsily. The girls probably responded in equally unsure ways. You didn't realize it at the time, but the girls in eighth grade were a mess of insecurities and surging hormones. Unfortunately, when the girls seemed to ignore you or react negatively to you, this left an indelible mark on your emotional brain.

Fast forward to the present day. You aren't the same naive, immature 13-year-old and neither are the women. Yet, your mind is probably stuck in early adolescence in terms of how you see yourself and women. Everything you internalized when you were an adolescent is probably still dictating your thoughts, feelings and actions. You still expect women to view you the same way they did when you were 13. And, you still expect them to react to you with the same adolescent immaturity they did when they were 13.

Because your mind is so powerful, you have found many creative ways to make sure these SLBs seem true. You've done it by drinking too much or packing on too much weight. Maybe you've worked too much, sat at home watching TV, or surfed the net instead of getting out around people. Maybe you've avoided talking to strangers altogether. Or maybe you've clumsily approached obviously unavailable women and then generalized that all women will reject you.

When your life seems to be proof of the validity of your thinking, the cycle just keeps spinning downward.

Your Mind Believes What Your Mind Tells Itself is True

Your mind can cause you great suffering. Your mind can also liberate you. Your mind can keep you stuck in the mire and your mind can help you attain everything you want in life. This is true because *your mind is the source of your feelings and the conductor of your actions.*

My cousin, Dr. Dannie Glover (he's a physician, not an actor) makes the following statement about the mind: "The mind resides in the brain and the brain is connected to every part of the body. Therefore, your mind controls everything about you through your brain."

The mind:

- Interprets the feelings generated in the primal part of the brain (fear, anxiety, etc.) and gives them a name and meaning.
- Creates feelings by what it thinks about and attunes itself to.
- Decides how to act upon feelings.
- Translates thoughts and feelings into physical responses (both positive and negative).

The mind can also:

- Be an observer of itself.
- Correct erroneous beliefs.
- Rewire old emotional programming.
- Soothe itself.
- Challenge itself.
- Grow beyond its own self-imposed limitations.

Your mind can enslave you and your mind can set you free. What this means is that your toxic shame, your self-limiting beliefs, and your outdated paradigms don't have to drive the bus of your life. You can take charge with your mind. You can take control of how you think. You can reshape your emotions. You can start acting in powerful ways that take you in the direction of getting what you want! This book will show you how!

Throughout this book, I am going to encourage you to do things that will stretch you outside of your comfort zone, and therefore make you anxious. It is in this *stretch zone* of life that you have the chance to become the most aware of your inner thoughts and beliefs. While in the stretch zone, you can consciously challenge your SLBs (lies) and replace them with more accurate information about you, women, and the world in general.

The Dating Essentials for Men Workbook contained in the Dating Essentials for Men Bonus Bundle presents some assignments to help you uncover and challenge your deeply held self-limiting beliefs. https:// datingessentialsformen.com/bonus-bundle/

CHAPTER 3: ELIMINATE YOUR FEAR OF REJECTION – FOREVER!

Rejection doesn't hurt.

As stated in the previous two chapters, self-limiting beliefs are the result of the inaccurate way you interpreted painful, frightening, or unpredictable experiences in childhood. *You believed these events were telling a story about you.*

Because the part of your brain responsible for conscious reasoning was fundamentally undeveloped in childhood, you had no way of knowing that these were inaccurate interpretations. As you have traveled through life, the paradigm effect strengthened these false beliefs. These beliefs have probably affected you in many areas – career, health, finances, friendships, happiness, relationships, and your sex life.

Ironically, the difficulty you have experienced with dating, relationships, and sex has not been the result of you being a worthless, unlovable loser. It is not the result of you being bald, too fat, too thin, too old, too young, too poor, or too short. Nor has it been the result of women being uncaring, gold-digging bitches. And, contrary to your distorted SLBs, women can't just look at you and sense that you are a loser.

Three Types of SLBs

There are three fundamental types of self-limiting beliefs – all of which can lead to self-criticism, inactivity, self-defeating behaviors, depression, procrastination, anxiety, no dates, and no sex. These three types of SLBs include: negative thoughts, distorted thoughts, and judgmental thoughts.

Negative thoughts might include:

- I don't deserve a loving relationship.
- I'm not good with small talk.
- I won't have anything interesting to say.
- Attractive women never talk to me.
- I'm not good with women.
- I'm afraid of rejection.
- I might fail and then I will look foolish.
- I'm too old.

Distorted thoughts include:

- If one woman rejects me, they will all reject me.
- All women are alike.
- Women don't like bald men.
- Women only go for guys with money.
- Rejection hurts.

Judgmental thoughts might include.

- I'm a fat slob.
- Women want successful men, not a loser like me.
- If I can't date a beautiful woman, I won't date.
- All women are gold-digging bitches.

Right now, I know some of you are thinking, "But some of my beliefs are true. Some are based on reality. I am short. I am shy. I don't make a lot of money. I am overweight. Women really do seem to be attracted to a different kind of guy than me. Women do keep telling me they just want to be friends."

While some of your SLBs might indeed have some truth to them, that is not the issue. Your real problem is this: *You will always act as if your SLBs are 100% TRUE!* You might be short, bald, and live with your parents, but *these realities will only become liabilities if you believe they are.*

Challenging Self-Limiting Beliefs

At one of my workshops for recovering Nice Guys in Mexico, a participant made the statement, "I'm afraid that if people see me sitting by myself on the beach drinking a Corona, they will think I'm a loser."

Over the course of the five-day workshop, this guy – who we'll call Diego – began to test and challenge his SLBs. He actually went and sat at a table on the beach by himself and drank some Coronas. Not only did no one seem to act negatively or judgmentally toward him, he had a really great time on the beach people watching and looking at the ocean.

Next, Diego decided to challenge his self-limiting beliefs even further by saying hello to people he met on the beach. Again, no one acted negatively toward him. In a short amount of time, he was starting conversations with strangers and approaching groups of women to test for interest. Again, no one judged him for being by himself on a beach in Mexico.

Diego continued challenging himself with no attachment to outcome. On the fourth day of the workshop, he started a conversation with an attractive young woman who sat down by herself at his favorite spot on the beach. At first, his SLBs screamed, "She's out of your league. She'll think you're intruding. She's hot, she probably has a boyfriend. She'll think you're a loser because you are all by yourself on the beach."

Diego decided to challenge the SLBs screaming in his head. He made a comment to the woman. She responded positively. He asked her to join him at his table. She did.

They began to talk. She was a physician on a short holiday. They spent the afternoon together. He invited her out to dinner. He kept challenging his SLBs and she kept responding with high interest. She ended up spending the entire night with him and they watched the sun come up together the next morning on the beach.

The following evening, while sharing his experience with the other guys in the workshop, he recounted his original SLB that people would judge him if he was sitting alone on the beach. While grinning from ear-to-ear he stated, "I guess I destroyed that myth!"

Blasting Your SLBs

People act consistently with their deepest held beliefs. We all act according to what we believe to be true – even if what we believe is limiting or self-destructive. If you believe you are worthless and that no one can love you, you will act accordingly. If you believe people will judge you, envy you, or criticize you if you are successful, you will act accordingly. If you believe you are a loser, you will act accordingly.

Your mind will not only see what it believes to be true, it will work hard to make sure what you experience feels familiar and consistent with previous experiences.

This chapter presents a number of powerful tools to help you identify the distorted and inaccurate thinking behind your self-limiting beliefs. It will also help you get them out of your head and replace them with more accurate, positive and productive beliefs. Part of this process will include showing you how to blast the fear of rejection – *the queen mother of all SLBs!*

Fear of Rejection

When I first started teaching classes on dating, I would tell my students to remove every form of the word *rejection* from their vocabulary. I would tell them that no woman has the power to reject them (i.e., to determine their value as a human being).

I would also make the point that just because one woman had low interest in them, that didn't mean that all women would feel the same. I would tell them that a woman wasn't rejecting them, she was just saying "no" to a date (or sex, or a relationship, etc.).

All of my students were banned from using the "R" word. I assumed that if I could change their vocabulary and eliminate such emotionally charged words, they might think differently and, subsequently, act differently. Unfortunately, just banning the word from their vocabulary didn't do a thing to change their behavior. Many of the guys would develop great skills but wouldn't apply them. They would still stay home, watch TV, surf the net – and avoid talking to women. Sure, they weren't using the word *rejection*. But, they weren't doing anything that might lead to getting there either.

Then, one day, one of my clients made a statement that made me rethink my approach to helping men deal with their fear of rejection. He stated that when a guy says he is afraid to talk to a woman because he might get rejected, he is just making an excuse. My wise client asserted, "Rejection doesn't hurt … but it is a great excuse to avoid facing the anxiety of talking to women."

I realized he was right. *Rejection doesn't hurt.* I've been *rejected* many times and it hasn't hurt me once. My internalized judgments and distortions might have beaten the hell out of me, but the actual rejection didn't hurt at all. It was just a "no" to a specific question. (low interest).

Rejection doesn't hurt. It is just what you tell yourself about the "no" that messes with your head. You will probably want to argue with me about how much it hurts to get rejected by a woman. I won't try and talk you out of this deeply held SLB. Instead, I suggest you test it.

Try an experiment: *Go out and get rejected at least three times this week.* Try to get three "noes" to date proposals from three strangers.

Treat dating as a science experiment, not as a way of validating your worth. One of the quickest, most powerful ways to blast away your SLBs is to consciously try to get to rejection as quickly as possible. Not only does this help you overcome your fear of rejection, but it also allows you to quickly move on to a woman who has high interest.

Ironically, *when you are trying to get to rejection quickly, it pretty much kills your fear and anxiety around getting rejected.* And, you won't actually get rejected as often as you might expect. I've had some students report that they couldn't complete the assignment because they received so many positive responses that they didn't have time to get three *actual* rejections.

Here is an example of the power of this approach: When he was in his 20s, Dr. Albert Ellis, the creator of *Rational Emotive Therapy* (RET), was deathly afraid of women and of being rejected by them. He decided to crush his fear of rejection by getting rejected by 200 women. During a two-week period, he approached 200 women and asked them to join him for dinner. All but one turned him down, and the one who accepted his date failed to show up! Although he didn't get one date, Dr. Ellis did conquer his fears of rejection and ultimately developed a robust social life!

He went on to write a column on relationships for *Penthouse Magazine* and into his 90s, still had a reputation of being a player.

The Magic Key

I have found that how a guy approaches this assignment is one of the biggest predictors of how well he will do in changing his SLBs and behavior. *The guys who challenge themselves and consciously seek rejection always experience an amazing transformation in their love lives.* This exercise seems to unlock the vault door to successful dating.

Even just thinking about trying to get three rejections will make you sweat. Your SLBs will scream at you. Don't listen to them. Calm your mind. Get out of the house and approach the first woman you see and tell her to give you her number so you can take her to coffee. Then do it again. And again.

Believe it or not, you might be hesitant to let go of your SLBs. They are part of your identity. They keep you feeling safe. They help you manage your anxiety. You might wonder, "Who will I be without them?" This can be frightening. This is why old habits are so hard to change. This is why you seem to act in ways that defeat your own best interests (addictions, not exercising, not saving money, gaining weight, etc.).

You may be short, bald, unemployed and live with your parents. But, that is not what limits you. It is what you believe about yourself that limits you. It is time to change your beliefs and change your life.

CHAPTER 4: DISCOVER THE POWER OF ABUNDANCE THINKING

If you can't see that you are already abundantly blessed, you won't be able to see it if it is multiplied by 10, or 100, or 1000, or even a million.

A while back, I received a voicemail from a client with whom I had worked on and off for a few years. In the message, his voice sounded desperate and strained.

"I need to schedule a session with you as soon as possible," he said. "I've been dating a great woman now for about a month. We've really hit it off and everything is going wonderfully. I'm following your rules. I only see her once a week. I'm staying off the phone with her. Everything is great. She thinks I'm wonderful and we always have a great time when we're together. I think this woman could be my Really Great Woman."

"There is only one problem," he continued. "I'm waiting for the other shoe to fall. I'm afraid I'm going to do something to blow it. I'm convinced it is only a matter of time until she sees through me and realizes I'm not so great. I know those are my self-limiting beliefs, but they haunt me constantly."

"What I want to talk with you about," he said, "is how can I learn to allow good things to happen to me without going into a panic about everything being taken away from me? I have to find a way to not shut down, imagining everything that can go wrong. I'm a wreck, I need to schedule an appointment as soon as I can."

This client is like many of the guys with whom I work on dating issues – riddled with fears that they will never find what they want, and if they do, it will quickly be taken away from them. When I talk with men about dating, love, and sex, I often hear many of the following kinds of statements:

- All the good women already have a boyfriend or they're married.
- You have to be rich, good looking, or have lots of confidence to get a good woman.
- If I do get a girlfriend, it will only be a matter of time until she will find a better man and leave me.
- I'll never find a good woman. I don't even know where to look.

These kinds of statements are examples of *deprivation thinking.*

When it comes to love and sex, most BDs not only see the glass as half empty, they see it as pretty much bone dry. Because of their deprivation view of the world, they can only see scarcity.

Here are some of the ways a deprivation view of the world might play out in your life:

- You stay home by yourself and spend time engaged in isolating activities.
- You avoid public places and rarely talk to people you don't know.
- You rarely interact with women you find attractive, and if you do, you project an aura of insecurity and neediness.
- If you do meet a woman, you immediately start seeking her approval and often become clingy and dependent.
- Once in a relationship, you either work way too hard to please your partner and/or you put up walls and become emotionally unavailable because you expect her to find a better man and leave.
- You frequently hold onto unsatisfying relationships way too long because you don't believe you can find another one that will be any better.

Deprivation thinking makes it difficult to get what you want in love and sex because it is difficult for you to see, and therefore accept, the abundance of the universe. If you think good women, good sex, and lasting love are in short supply, why would you put yourself out there? Why risk rejection and disappointment?

Because of your deprivation thinking, you don't notice all of the doors of opportunity that open up to you. And, you certainly don't walk through them. You end up playing it safe, doing the same old thing, staying home and avoiding situations that might put you into contact with women. All the while you probably envy other guys who seem to get all the breaks and have all the luck.

Why You Don't Believe There is Enough to Go Around

Your deprivation view of yourself and relationships are a direct result of a life paradigm developed in childhood. When your childhood needs were not met in a timely, consistent manner, you came to see the world as an unpredictable, lonely place. You probably saw the things you needed most (love, attention, affection, etc.) as being in short supply or only going to other people. These experiences created a view of the world defined by lack.

Now, as an adult, you make a distorted comparison between yourself and others around you. This means you typically see other men getting all the good-looking women, the sex, and the fulfilling relationships. These comparisons result in envy, resentment, and, more often than not, an unconscious surrender to what seems like the harsh unfairness of the world around you.

An Abundant World

Here's the good news – *the world you live in is different from the family in which you were raised!* There is an abundance of goodies out there and there is plenty for everyone. Around the world, men of all ages, races, nationalities, and walks of life are enjoying love, sex and amazing relationships. This alone is proof that there is plenty out there.

The men who find the things you are looking for are no different than you. They're not better looking, smarter, funnier, richer, or in better shape. When a seemingly average guy gets a great woman, there's only one difference between him and you: He has a worldview that allows him to see himself as worthy of love and he is open to letting it into his life.

The world is filled with unlimited opportunities. There is an abundance that is freely available to you. There are boatloads of goodies (great women, great sex, great relationships) out there just waiting for you. This is the reality of the world in which you live. Deprivation thinking blinds you to the beauty and bounty of this world. Abundance thinking opens your eyes to it.

The premise of this chapter is twofold:

- *The world is an abundant place.*
- *You have been and will continue to be abundantly blessed.*

The problem you have around finding love, sex and a great relationship has nothing to do with the supply side of things in the world. The problem is what was programmed into your brain when you were a small child. *The problems you have around finding what you want in love and sex is not a problem of scarcity, but with the perception of scarcity!*

Opening up to Abundance

In 2002, I wrote a series of lessons based on my book, *No More Mr. Nice Guy*, for an online class on work and career. One of the lessons was on the subject of abundance. Initially, it proved to be one of the most difficult lessons I'd ever written. Intellectually, I could think of what to write on the subject, but emotionally, I was blocked. This emotional block showed up in my writing. I realized that my own deprivation thinking, programmed in childhood, was getting in the way of writing about abundance with emotional clarity. I realized that before I could write believably about abundance, I had to be tuned into it in my own life.

I decided to try an experiment. I asked a friend to join me in an abundance practice. We agreed that every day, we would kneel next to our beds first thing in the morning and last thing at night and think about the things for which we were grateful. We committed to do this together because we both knew that this would involve changing some pretty deep-seated emotions and ways of thinking. We were right.

We both got off to a good start, but started slipping within a few days. We occasionally missed our morning or evening sessions. Even though we were both experiencing greater peace of mind and happiness from the ritual, our minds found ways to help us "forget" to do what was making us feel so good. Additionally, we both noticed that within a few days, our minds began to battle with us. A civil war had begun.

The part of our minds that always thought about the world in terms of lack and loss was deeply entrenched. Our new abundance and gratitude thinking was challenging the status quo. This created *emotional and cognitive dissonance*. Nevertheless, we persisted with our new practice of daily gratitude.

In a short amount of time, we both noticed internal changes. We worried less. We were happier. We didn't dwell on past losses or mistakes and didn't obsess about future disasters. We didn't resent or envy other people's blessings. Judgment waned. Joy increased. We both began to experience an inner peace, knowing that everything would work out just fine, even if we didn't know how.

We came to the awareness that our needs had been taken care of every day of our lives up until then. Why would that change tomorrow? Through a daily gratitude practice, some other important facts about abundance came to us:

- Abundance isn't a pursuit; it is a state of mind.
- Abundance isn't an issue of degree, it's an issue of awareness and acceptance.
- Abundance is not defined by how much a person has, but by how aware a person is of how much he has.
- Abundance is like air. You are already experiencing it with every breath you take. If you already have all the air you need, there is no reason to hold your breath and hoard the air you have, gasp for more air, worry if there will be enough air tomorrow, or envy those who appear to be breathing more than their fair share.

This practice of gratitude changed my life and continues to do so today. Whenever I find myself worried, uptight, anxious, or thinking negatively, I pause and think about all the things I am grateful for in life.

Within moments I feel calm. The world seems like a friendly, inviting place again.

I now walk through more open doors because I see them more clearly and I believe it is okay for me to experience abundance. Abundance thinking has replaced the deprivation thinking that used to control my view of the world and of myself. As a result, I am constantly amazed at all the great people, things, and experiences that flood into my life. At times, *I feel like a walking miracle magnet.*

Abundance surrounds you. You have all that you need to be completely happy, right now. Creating an abundance mentality not only opens you up to recognize how blessed you are right now, it makes you more aware of the many open doors of opportunity that surround you. Abundance thinking also gives you the courage to walk through these open doors and experience the adventure of living in this wonderful world.

The rest of this chapter presents a number of things that you can do to increase your abundance awareness and break free from old, deprivation ways of seeing the world. These suggestions aren't magic, but if you practice them regularly, they can change your life in ways you never expected.

In my experience, developing an abundance mentality is the most powerful way to naturally attract really great women to you – without having to learn silly pickup lines, magic tricks, or hypnosis!

Develop a Daily Gratitude Practice

Develop a daily routine of thinking about things for which you feel grateful. Pick a time at least once or twice a day when you can focus on these things. It only takes two or three minutes. I like doing it right before going to bed or right after getting up. You can do it when you brush your teeth, while you sit at stop lights, or during any other daily routine. Make it a habit by practicing it consistently over time. Ask a friend or family member to do the same.

I know several people who keep a gratitude stone in their pocket. Every time they put their hand in their pocket and touch the stone or remove it from their pocket, they think about things for which they are grateful.

It won't do any good for the universe to multiply your blessings a hundred-fold if you aren't already aware of how blessed you are. *You already have everything you need.* Focus on that, rather than what you don't have now or didn't receive in the past.

Here's an example: A few years ago, I began a gratitude practice that focused on the special way every significant person in my life has blessed me. I started this practice because I noticed that I had been obsessing about all the ways the people in my life (parents, girlfriends, friends, wives) had loved me less than perfectly. Not only did this thinking make me feel bad and cheated, but it was also getting reinforced in my life.

I decided instead to attune myself to how all these people had uniquely loved me. I focused on at least one unique gift every significant person in my life has given me. Not only did my overall mood change, it changed how I perceived these people, and it began to attract people to me who could love me more completely than those in the past could.

Practice Receiving

Receiving is probably inconsistent with your beliefs about yourself and the world. If you don't believe your needs are important, you won't be receptive to the good things the world wants to give you. In order to experience the abundance of the world, you have to practice being a good receiver.

If you aren't comfortable receiving, you will never get what you want (this seems like a pretty straight-forward principle, but it is amazing how your mind will fight against it). For example, if you want a girlfriend or great sex, you have to be open to receiving these things. Receiving takes practice.

Try this: Every day this week, ask three people to do three things for you that you can do yourself. As you do this, lean into the anxiety. Listen to the chatter in your mind that resists asking and receiving. Use affirmations to calm the anxiety.

Change What Your Mind Attunes Itself To

Current brain research has revealed that your mind has thousands of thought impulses every moment. You aren't conscious of most of them. They are like the constant noises in your daily life that your mind learns to minimize or filter out. This is good news. You would go crazy if every thought impulse made it into consciousness simultaneously.

Over time, your mind has attuned itself to the thoughts that most closely reflect your deepest held beliefs about yourself and the world. These thoughts arise from your emotional core, and become the familiar, well-worn, neural goat paths of your consciousness.

The good news is the human mind is capable of choosing to attune itself to whatever thought impulses it wants. It is extremely difficult for the mind to attune itself to contradictory thoughts at the same time (though the mind is capable of entertaining conflicting thoughts or beliefs within milliseconds of each other – "she loves me; she loves me not.") In general, your mind would prefer to stick with one type of thought over time.

If your mind is in the habit of thinking negatively, it will do it consistently and instinctively. It is almost impossible to make yourself quit thinking negatively because negative thoughts will always make up a certain percentage of what is bouncing around in your mind at any given time. If your mind feels at home with negative thoughts, it will want to keep going back to familiar territory. The only way to change negative or deprivation thinking is to consciously attune yourself to positive or abundant thoughts. And you don't have to make them up. They are already there.

A gratitude practice is a powerful way to attune yourself to different types of thought impulses in your mind. By regularly thinking about things for which you are grateful, for example, your mind will begin to attune to other thought impulses that are consistent with this type of thinking. Thought impulses that are contrary, tend to go unnoticed.

Challenge What Your Mind Believes to Be True

Your mind believes what your mind tells itself is true. The paradigm effect ensures that you will find evidence to support your beliefs. Your mind will make sure that your thoughts become reality. Your mind determines your reality. What you think about is what you will attract and create. If your mind dwells on what you don't want, that is what you will attract to yourself. If you focus on how lonely you are, what you lack, how angry you are, how badly women have hurt you, etc., that is what you will attract.

If you believe all women are angry, needy, liars, gold-diggers, incapable of fidelity, etc., these are the only traits you will see in women (you won't notice all the women who don't possess these traits). You will attract these kinds of women, and this is the only kind of woman with whom you will be comfortable.

If you believe you are unattractive and uninteresting, you'll never be receptive to a really great woman coming into your life. If you do bump into one, your mind will convince you this is a fluke and she will soon find out what a loser you are. Your mind will find creative ways to push her away in order to make your outer reality fit your inner beliefs.

I have worked with many men who have been cheated on a number of times. These men are now certain beyond a shadow of a doubt that they will be cheated on by all women who come into their lives. Consequently, they tend to attract women who can't be faithful. If they do find a good woman, these men put up so many emotional walls, that in time, even a woman who has never cheated before eventually responds to the attention of another man. This reinforces both the beliefs and the reality of these men.

The only way to change reality is to change your thinking. This doesn't mean you have to develop a Pollyanna way of viewing the world. It does mean changing the way you think so you can change the way you see the world.

Expect a Miracle

Every relationship is a miracle. Every time you leave your house and talk to another person, you open the door for the miraculous. Very few amazing things happen when you are sitting home by yourself – miracles happen in the context of people.

Abundance thinking opens you up to miracles. The more time you spend outside your house talking to people, the more you increase the potential for great things to happen. I anticipate some kind of miracle every time I walk out my front door. I am constantly amazed at the truly unexpected encounters, events, and opportunities that occur in my life almost daily.

You can't make miracles happen, but you can put yourself in a position to let them happen. Just as luck favors the prepared mind, miracles happen to the guy who gets out of his house and talks to people everywhere he goes! The greatest miracles typically happen when we least expect them. This is called, *serendipity* – "finding what you weren't looking for."

How many of your most memorable life experiences were the result of serendipity – a new friendship, a great day, a new girlfriend, an unexpected sexual opportunity? The more you become conscious of the abundance in the world, the more likely you are to recognize and walk through open doors. When you walk through open doors you change your core beliefs about yourself and the world. The more you embrace abundance, the more you will see abundance. The more you see abundance, the more you will walk through the open doors.

The result is that you begin to see the world as a bountiful place filled with opportunities for great love, great sex, and great relationships with some really great women! You live in an abundant world. Get out and enjoy it!

CHAPTER 5: OVERCOME YOUR ANXIETY WITH WOMEN

Thinking causes anxiety, acting cures it.

When I began teaching dating skills to men, I noticed that many of the guys who attended my classes and seminars applied the skills I taught them with great success. At the same time, other men in these same programs resisted applying the skills and continued to feel frustrated about their love lives. This puzzled me.

Why did some men apply the information with great success while others didn't? After pondering this issue for a while, I realized the problem wasn't what it seemed on the surface. The roadblock for these men wasn't a lack of knowledge or skills. It wasn't an inability to apply what they had learned. *The problem was a fear of success.* These resistant guys realized that their new skills and insights would actually work, and this scared the bejeezus out of them. Let me explain.

Your mind is like the board of a large corporation. The board is made up of many voting members. Some of these members exert more influence than others. The most powerful members of the board have one goal and one goal only – to avoid having to experience the anxiety of the unknown. The goal of these powerful mental board members is to keep you doing things the way that you have always done them. Even if this behavior perpetuates feelings of frustration and loneliness, it helps you avoid the anxiety of the unknown.

For example, if I gave you the assignment to say hello to three strangers a day, your mind would experience an immediate and overwhelming panic. This is because this is a new behavior with unknown outcomes.

Here is the way the powerful board members in your mind would spring into action if I gave you this assignment. They would approach another board member, mention how much work you need to get done, and suggest there really isn't time to approach three strangers and talk to them. Your board members would lobby another board member and remind him how tired you are right now, and that it's probably a good idea to stay home tonight, surf the internet, and relax.

The other mental board members are often quick to agree and vote for these proposals, not realizing that the primary agenda is not the one being voted on. The real, unspoken goal is to avoid doing anything new and unknown that would lead to discomfort, fear and anxiety. So instead of talking to three strangers (which will cause anxiety), you decide it is more important to take it easy or get some more work done (it doesn't really matter what as long it provides an effective distraction from the anxiety of the unknown).

Fear of Success

Success is scary. Your mind is much more comfortable hanging out in the same old familiar neighborhood than it is venturing into the unknown. Your mind will do all it can to keep you doing the same familiar things over and over again, even if these things are causing pain and frustration, and don't take you where you want to go. Doing things that might lead to success into new uncharted territories. Yes, your *hood* might really suck, but you know your way around.

Applying the principles I teach in *Dating Essentials for Men will greatly increase the likelihood of* your dating success. While this may sound like good news, what it really means is a ten-fold increase in the anxiety factor.

Magic Bullets

Here is an interesting discovery I've made about bad daters – they love techniques. If you are like most BDs, you believe that there is some opener, some pickup line, some magic trick that will miraculously make women attracted to you (especially the women you find most attractive). You might have purchased this book and ordered numerous other dating and pickup products looking for that one magic bullet.

This phenomenon is the result of not understanding the real reason for your dating and mating frustration. You have probably spent years analyzing why women don't seem to be attracted to you. You have attributed it to things like not being good looking enough, not having interesting things to say, or just being a fucked-up loser. Maybe you've blamed the women.

Your mind has settled on one or more of these dynamics to explain your bad luck with women. Your mind then goes out and finds loads of evidence to support these belief systems. This is why you believe that finding some super powerful pickup technique will allow you to overcome all of these supposed limitations on your ability to attract women. Funny thing is, no matter how many approaches or pickup lines you hear or read about, you're still sitting at home on Friday night researching shit on the web that you'll probably never buy.

What's the problem? The problem is, *you've misdiagnosed the disease*. What if you went to the doctor suffering from a sinus infection and he gave you medicine to treat jock itch? No matter how religiously you applied the jock itch powder, your sinus infections would linger on. Get the point?

By misdiagnosing your dating ills, you've kept seeking the wrong cure for what ails you. More techniques will only make you what I call, a *geek with techniques*. No matter how many pickup lines, openers, and *negs* you memorize, you'll still find yourself stuck in the same old frustrating place. The only remedy seems to be continuing your search for the one magic bullet that will turn your luck around.

Here's the real problem: The idea of approaching women, talking to them, getting phone numbers, and eventually taking them to bed – all make you anxious. The real reason you aren't out dating and getting laid right now is not one of the reasons you've probably convinced yourself of. The real reason is *FEAR AND ANXIETY*.

That's it. Your dating frustration isn't the result of you being too busy, too old, too fat, too poor, too ugly, etc. Nor is it the result of all women being flakes. It is the result of you being scared. If you go out and apply all the techniques you've learned, you would actually have to interact with women and talk to them. Then, you might end up dating them and sleeping with them. Even though your mind thinks you would love for these things to happen, you really don't.

Success is scary. Because having a great girlfriend or great sex is outside the norm of your past experience, these things make you anxious. The possibility of really getting what you want makes your palms sweat and knees knock. Because you don't like feeling anxious, you never apply all the dating skills and pickup techniques you've spent time and money studying.

Managing Anxiety vs. Soothing Anxiety

BDs spend a lot of time doing something I call *anxiety management.* Anxiety management is the ongoing, often unconscious attempt to prevent uncomfortable feelings.

It usually takes the form of:

- Avoidance
- Isolation
- Procrastination
- Playing it safe
- Avoiding risks
- Doing the same old thing over and over again

Like most BDs, you probably spend a lot of time and energy trying to manage your anxiety by avoiding doing things that might take you into unknown or uncharted territory. *Your mind would rather manage old, familiar anxieties than confront new and unknown ones.* Managing anxiety may keep you stuck in all kinds of unhappy, dead-end – even painful situations – but as they say, "the devil you know is better than the devil you don't."

Anxiety management focuses on trying to control people, situations, and things outside of you. In contrast, *soothing anxiety* is an internal process. Self-soothing is calming the anxiety inside of you instead of trying to manage events outside of you. It involves you consciously leaning into fear while calming yourself from within. Managing anxiety keeps you stuck. Soothing anxiety sets you free.

Let me tell you a secret. All men experience some degree of anxiety when interacting with women, especially women they find attractive. This is normal. Our goal isn't to make this anxiety go away. If you are like most BDs, you have spent a lot of time and energy since adolescence trying to find a way to approach desirable women without having to feel any anxiety. As a result, you have probably tried to manage your anxiety in a couple of ways.

The first has been avoiding women altogether. You might have gone out with women who approached you first, or you might have dated down. But your anxiety has prevented you from interacting with women to whom you are attracted.

A second is by becoming a girlfriend with a penis. A girlfriend with a penis is the guy who becomes a woman's friend because his anxiety prevents him from coming on too strong or doing something that might scare her off. He spends lots of time listening to her complain about her "jerk" boyfriend. He'll volunteer to help her sister move. He'll be on call 24/7 to help her solve her problems. All the while he hopes that someday, she'll see what a great guy he is and want to date him and/or sleep with him. Unfortunately, this strategy is terrible foreplay and it does nothing to turn a woman on or make her think about dating the guy who is so eager to do whatever it takes to make her happy.

Not only will these strategies fail to diminish your anxiety, but they will also prevent you from getting what you want. In order to date successfully, you have to learn to calm your anxious mind. Learning to soothe anxiety is the single most effective way to improve your dating skills and get the love and sex you want.

Anxiety is real. But it won't kill you. Instead of waiting for the anxiety to go away, this chapter will teach you how to soothe it from within while you venture into the unknown.

Change Your Thinking

One of the most effective ways to soothe your anxiety is to change the basic message your mind is telling you about the things you fear. In the book *Feel the Fear and Do it Anyway,* Susan Jeffers asserts that all fear is the result of your mind telling you "I can't handle it." Your mind is convinced that you can't handle things like rejection, looking foolish, being found out, getting dumped, or having to break-up.

Because your mind believes what your mind tells you, you are convinced that you really can't handle these things. Dr. Jeffers asserts that one of the most effective ways to calm your mind is to consciously replace these lies with the truth – *You CAN handle it!*

Think about this: You have handled everything so far in life (even when you didn't believe you could) – you will handle everything else that comes your way. "I can handle it" is one of the most powerful self-soothing techniques you can use. Even when your negative self-limiting beliefs are screaming at you, you can calm your anxious mind by repeating to yourself: "I can handle it. No matter what happens, I'll handle it."

For example, when you are interacting with a woman whom you find attractive, your anxiety level will begin to skyrocket. The powerful board members of your mind immediately go into action to get your anxiety back down. They start whispering to the other board members, "She's out of your league," "You'll be intruding," or "She probably has a boyfriend."

Because your mind doesn't like feeling anxious, and asking this woman out could lead to all kinds of unexpected results, you believe all the things your mind tells you. You either don't ask her out or you ask her indirectly and nothing ever happens. (To the board members of your mind, this is success!)

Here is what you can do to soothe your anxiety enough to approach this woman. Talk back to your mental board of directors. Say to your board members: "That may all be true, but I can handle it." As you interact with a woman you find attractive, keep repeating to yourself, "I can handle it." Repeat it as many times as is necessary to keep you moving forward.

Remember, your goal is not to make your anxiety go away. Your goal is to move forward EVEN when you are feeling anxious. It is amazing how simply repeating, "I can handle it" will help you move forward and take action in situations that would have previously kept you frozen.

Stop Thinking and Start Acting

Since your mind is a problem-solving machine, you analyze and think a lot. Unfortunately, the more you think and ruminate about something, the more your mind becomes paralyzed with *what ifs* and anxiety. Have you ever noticed that the more you think about a particular situation or a particular woman, the more your anxiety goes up and the more you avoid doing anything?

Here's some good news: *thinking causes anxiety, but acting cures it.* One of the most powerful ways to soothe your anxiety is to not let your mind freak itself out by thinking too much. If there is something you need to do, do it now! That's the most effective way to bust anxiety. Act!

Let's say you are standing in line in a coffee shop and an attractive woman is standing next to you. Or, you are in a club and a woman looks your way and smiles. Don't wait. Don't think too much about it. Follow the *3-second rule.* If you think about approaching a woman, do it in 3 seconds or less. Waiting longer to act will give you too much time to think about everything that might go wrong. Subsequently, you'll get uptight and won't do anything.

Here's another rule: *You can't spend more time thinking about a woman than you have actually spent with her.* Many BDs think obsessively about some woman whom they have never actually met or dated. Sometimes, this woman doesn't even know the guy exists. This is a waste of time and creates tons of unnecessary anxiety.

Waiting for anxiety to go away so you can interact with women will never happen. The only way to bust the anxiety is to repeatedly interact with them. And just for the record, *attractive women make all men nervous.* It is amazing how much your anxiety will begin to abate once you stop thinking so much and start acting.

This is why all of the tools and assignments in *Dating Essentials for Men* are geared toward getting you to *act.* The more you act, the more confident and comfortable you will become with doing things outside your comfort zone. So, stop thinking and start acting!

Treat Dating Like a Scientific Experiment

When you interact with a woman whom you find attractive, you have already given her a certain amount of power to *accept* or *reject* you. That's why you have anxiety. A great way to soothe this anxiety is to look at dating as a *scientific experiment.* Instead of interacting with women hoping you don't get rejected, try interacting with them and experimenting with what seems to effectively get their attention and what doesn't. Don't worry about outcomes. Be a good scientist. Just observe responses.

Keep a tally of high and low interest responses. Don't take anything a woman does personally. She's just a subject in your research study. This attitude helps lower your anxiety and increases the likelihood that you will interact with women more naturally, boldly, and effectively.

For example, talk to women and ask them a poll question just to see how they respond. Practice teasing women and observe their reaction. Kiss women on the cheek to see if it seems to increase their interest level. Do it in the name of science. When you test for interest with no attachment to outcome, you will take more risks, appear more confident, and interact with a lot more women. So, put on your lab coat, grab your clipboard, and get going.

Soothe Your Anxiety, Don't Manage It

Anxiety is a part of life. It won't kill you! As long as you are moving forward in life and pushing your edge, you will experience anxiety. Everyone does. *If you feel a little bit excited and a little bit scared, it is a sign that you are alive and kicking and challenging yourself.*

To blast your dating anxiety, practice the following basic social skills every day:

- Consciously expand your route. Go places you don't regularly go. Get out and be around people.
- Ask people you don't know how their day is going so far (men, women, children, etc.).

- Make eye contact with and smile at people (men, women, children, etc.).
- Start a conversation with someone you don't know (man or woman).
- Get to rejection quickly.

While you are doing these things every day:

- Practice soothing your anxiety rather than managing it.
- Feel your fear and do it anyway.
- Lean into anxiety.
- Welcome the opportunity to blast away your self-limiting beliefs.
- Don't give up.
- Don't let one bad experience or one rejection inhibit you.
- Don't take one woman's rejection as proof that you are a loser and will never find love.
- Keep at it until it feels second nature.
- Most importantly, have fun.

Chapter 6 presents more self-soothing techniques to help you follow through on the suggestions above.

CHAPTER 6: TAKE A BREATH AND SOOTHE YOURSELF

Breathe up through your asshole.

This chapter presents a number of techniques you can use to soothe yourself anytime you feel anxious. Any time you get outside of your comfort zone, you will feel some degree of anxiety. This is normal. This is what life is about. As long as you are growing and challenging yourself, anxiety will be a familiar companion. Remember, we aren't trying to eliminate anxiety. In fact, the goal is to learn how to effectively soothe your anxiety as you take bold action in life.

Breathe Using Your Diaphragm

Diaphragmatic breathing is the healthiest way to breathe and is a first step in normalizing your nervous system in order to soothe anxiety or panic symptoms. It is the most natural way to breathe. Observe how a very young baby breathes – they will use their diaphragm/belly with each breath.

Years of poor posture, anxious thinking, tension and pressure will usually result in breathing patterns which are less than ideal, and commonly involve:

Rapid, upper chest breathing, leading to →

Over-breathing, leading to →

Depletion of carbon dioxide stores.

Relearning to use your diaphragm in breathing and to reduce your rate of breathing is an important first step in soothing the symptoms of anxiety, anger, panic, etc. Upper chest, rapid breathing gets rid of too much carbon dioxide causing us to feel agitated and breathless. It causes our nervous system to go into overdrive. To check how you are breathing:

- Rest one hand on your upper chest and the other over your navel area.
- Breathe normally for a minute or so.
- Notice which hand rises first when you inhale.

If the upper hand rises first, you are using upper chest breathing. If the lower hand rises first you are breathing with your diaphragm. If both move at the same time you are using a mix of both.

Spend a few minutes a couple of times a day practicing using your diaphragm:

- Sit in an upright position looking straight ahead. You can close your eyes if it helps you to concentrate on the process.
- Put one palm on your upper chest and the other over your navel. (Your objective is to have the lower hand rise *first* when you breathe in.)
- Breathe out gently and effortlessly. Now wait for a second or two until the body spontaneously begins the inhalation – this will occur naturally, of its own accord.
- Allow the air to naturally flow in again until it stops, again of its own accord. Make no effort whatsoever to deepen the inhalation. You are allowing your body to find its own natural rate of breathing. Relaxing into the process, allow your breathing to slow down and become more and more shallow.
- Continue doing this for about 4-5 minutes.
- Hint: Pretend you are breathing up through your asshole!

Whenever you feel stressed (or anytime you think about it), take a moment and slowly take a few breaths from deep down in your diaphragm. Notice how you immediately feel calmer and your mind slows down.

Visualize Positive Results

Your mind is a *problem-solving machine*. When presented with a problem or challenge, it will predict and analyze every possible outcome – positive and negative. In most social situations, your mind will do this in a split second. Unfortunately, your mind can't tell the difference between real and perceived outcomes. It treats them all the same and believes they are all equally possible. Your mind creates its own reality based on what it can imagine. These imagined outcomes are often influenced by SLBs and past experiences.

In addition, your mind doesn't distinguish well between past, present, and future. Imagined future outcomes feel exactly the same and carry the same weight as experiences from the past and present. Your mind can't tell the difference between a well-imagined thought and reality.

The brighter and/or more creative you are, the more possible outcomes to any situation your mind can imagine. Because you can easily imagine all the possible negative outcomes of any personal endeavor, you get overwhelmed and typically do nothing. Your creative mind is extremely capable of creating lurid, nightmare scenarios and negative consequences to pretty much every new or unfamiliar life situation. I call all of these possible negative outcomes *trap doors.*

- What if she has a boyfriend and he beats me up?
- If I approach a woman, I probably won't be able to think of anything interesting to say and she'll walk away.
- What if she thinks I'm intruding? I hate it when people intrude on me.
- What if we go out and I end up breaking up with her and she goes ballistic?
- What if I can't satisfy her in bed and she leaves me for another man?

Whether you realize it or not, your mind is extremely effective at creating trap doors. Since your mind tells you these things could happen, your mind believes they will. Your mind creates so many possible negative scenarios that no matter which way you go, you see potential trap doors awaiting you. Why not visualize positive results instead? Since your mind will believe anything you tell it, it will assume that what you are telling it is true.

Here's an example of the power of visualizing positive results: Researchers divided basketball teams into two groups. They had the first group shoot 100 free throws at the end of every practice. They had the second group simply visualize shooting 100 free throws at the end of every practice. Of course, the second group never missed a shot in their visualization. The first group missed several actual shots. When it came to game situations, the second group actually made a higher percentage of their free throws than the first group. That's the power of visualization!

Instead of rerunning old scenarios of rejection and past failures whenever you think about interacting with women, visualize success. Create a visual in your mind of women smiling and responding positively when you interact with them. Keep visualizing until your mind becomes comfortable with these outcomes.

Practice this: Visualize a woman you find attractive but have never interacted with in a direct way. See yourself interacting with her and asking her out for coffee. See the smile on her face as she replies, "I'd love to." Repeat this until you overcome the resistance in your mind (remember, even in fantasy, your mind wants to hold on to its old ways of protecting you from anxiety). I encourage you to visualize this scene several times a day until this scenario actually becomes plausible to the board members in your mind.

Stop Trying to Figure Out Why Women Do What They Do

Several years ago, when my stepson was in his early teens, he was watching a teen drama on television. One of the female characters on the show was creating all kinds of emotional turmoil – drama. In frustration, he turned to his fourteen-year-old sister and asked, "Why do girls do that?" His sister, in all of her adolescent female wisdom replied, "How the hell would I know? I don't know why I do what I do half the time!"

Most people don't know why they do what they do. Most behavior is controlled by unconscious factors. It is a waste of time to try and figure out why people do what they do. Bad daters spend way too much time trying to figure women out. They often ask, "Why did she do that?" I usually respond with "Who the hell knows and why do you care?"

Don't analyze women. Don't try and figure them out. You have no idea what is going on in their lives or in their minds. Their behavior has nothing to do with you. As David Deida, the author of *The Way of the Superior Man* puts it, "They are the weather." A woman either has high interest in you or she has low interest. It isn't personal either way. Don't try and figure out why.

For example, a while back I left a restaurant with a group of friends. Several people were standing outside about to enter. I approached one of the women in a friendly manner. She was abrupt and turned away. I started to walk away when she turned back to me and said, "I'm sorry, we're in the middle of a crisis here. My friend just lost her wallet." Then, the woman proceeded to chat with me for several minutes and introduced me to some of her friends. If I had taken her initial behavior personally or tried to figure it out, I would have completely misinterpreted her response.

When you stop trying to figure out why people do what they do, your anxiety level will go down. When you quit taking things personally and realize that what women do has much less to do with you than you imagine, you'll be able to interact with them with more confidence and less anxiety. And, this will increase your likelihood of success.

Get to Rejection Quickly

Most BDs interact with women hoping to not get rejected. This is like going to bat in baseball and hoping you don't strike out. It will make you timid, guarded and anxious. It is better to get into the batter's box looking for a pitch that you can take a good cut at. It relaxes you and helps you do your best.

As I proposed in Chapter 3, trying to get rejected is one of the most effective ways to calm anxiety when interacting with women. If you are looking for the one technique that will revolutionize your dating, this is it. This is the nuclear bomb that will obliterate your anxiety and turn you into a true dating machine!

Since you are trying to get rejected, you have nothing to fear when you interact with a woman. If you have nothing to fear, you act more confidently. This will allow you to take more chances. By taking more chances, more doors open up to you. This cycle repeats itself over and over.

Whenever you find yourself feeling anxious about interacting with women in general or a specific woman, tell yourself, "Okay, let's see if I can get her to reject me." Then lean into the anxiety and see how quickly you can get to rejection. Not only does this lower your anxiety, but it will also lead to a lot of women responding with unexpected high interest!

CHAPTER 7: USE THE SECRET WOMEN DON'T WANT YOU TO KNOW TO YOUR ADVANTAGE

A woman's greatest asset is a man's imagination. – Anne Corio

Odds are, a primary reason you are reading this book is that you have an unrealistic and unsubstantiated fantasy about women and what they can do for you. If you are like most BDs, your distorted beliefs about women create several problems for you. These distorted beliefs:

- Make you anxious around women.
- Make it more difficult for you to approach women and talk to them.
- Make you care way too much what women think about you.
- Force you to hide your perceived *faults* from women which makes it impossible for you to be honest and transparent.
- Make women seem powerful and unattainable.
- Create feelings of helplessness, rage, and resentment toward women.
- Keep you from setting the tone and taking the lead with women.
- Make it difficult for you to have an intimate relationship with women.

Many of your distorted beliefs about women are the result of a feminine mythology that permeates our culture. Literature, poetry, music, movies, advertising, pornography – all create the image that women are objects of mystery and desire. If you have bought into these beliefs and stereotypes, welcome to the club.

On one hand, this feminine mythology does a disservice to both men and women. The myths actually get in the way of women finding the deep connection that they crave with men. The mythology also keeps men confused, insecure, and anxious around women. Neither of these situations serve women or men well. On the other hand, men seem to enjoy the feminine mythology because it gives them a seemingly wonderful prize to pursue – a prize they believe will transform and complete their lives when attained. I suspect that some women also like the idea of being seen as mysterious and special.

Even though most women know beyond a shadow of a doubt that they are not special or mysterious, many have bought into the mythology and believe it is an essential part of attracting and keeping a man.

What is the secret that women are afraid of you finding out about them (and all the while, deep down hoping you do)? It is this: *Women are nothing more than imperfect human beings!* As mysterious or special as these feminine creatures may seem, *they are just wounded creatures walking the planet.*

I don't mean this in a derogatory way. We are all imperfect. But, it is interesting how some men respond when I make this statement about the female gender. I've actually had some guys verbally attack me for making such a "demeaning" statement about women. Therefore, it is important for me to make clear that referring to women as "wounded creatures" or "imperfect human beings" isn't demeaning, it is loving.

When you clear out your distorted beliefs and take women down off the pedestal, you can actually have healthy, balanced relationships with them. This process allows you to let go of rage, resentment, anxiety, and feelings of helplessness. It lets you really get to know women and find out if you like them for who they are. So, from this point of view, it is respectful to "demystify" these seemingly mysterious beings.

Ironically, when I tell women how men tend to put them (especially the good-looking ones) on a pedestal, they are surprised. The typical female response is: "you're kidding, why do they do that?" A healthy woman doesn't want to be on a pedestal and doesn't want men to be intimidated by her. Healthy women are smart enough to know that this works against them. Most women want to be seen and judged for who they are – perfectly imperfect human beings.

In order to relate to women as people and to create truly intimate, mature relationships with them, we have to explode some of the myths that surround them. By exposing and exploding the following five myths about women, my goal is to help you see women more clearly. As you come to see women as they are, you increase the possibility of getting what you want in love, sex and relationships.

Myth #1: Women are Inherently Superior to Men

When you listen to bad daters talk about women, you would assume that members of the opposite sex are the most evolved, self-aware creatures imaginable. While some women do indeed have their stuff together, this doesn't explain the universal awe that many men have for women (especially attractive women).

BDs believe they must hide every flaw from these seemingly perfect beings. These men assume that the majority of women are so secure and evolved that they would never be interested in someone as lowly and imperfect as them (even when it is obvious these same women have tons of baggage).

Ironically, in Western culture, it is actually safer to assume that the average woman has a fairly low opinion of herself and has plenty of emotional baggage. For example, a primary source of esteem for women in this culture is physical appearance. Since childhood, most women have been comparing themselves to every other woman. As a result, many women are excessively self-critical.

Just look at the standards of beauty that women are expected to attain in Western culture. Even the most beautiful woman can look around and find 10 women more beautiful than her. These unrealistic standards of beauty are a primary reason many women have low self-esteem, eating disorders, and body distortions. It's why there is a multi-billion-dollar fashion and beauty industry. It's also why women constantly ask the question: "Do these jeans make my ass look fat?"

In addition to unrealistic standards of beauty, other factors affect self-esteem in women. Statistically, one in three women in the United States will be sexually abused before she reaches age 18. Sexual abuse creates all kinds of emotional turmoil for survivors. It doesn't make them damaged goods, but it does affect their mood and self-esteem, as well as their ability to relate with men in a healthy way. For various reasons, women have more mood disorders than men. They have higher incidences of depression, anxiety, borderline personality and psychosomatic disorders. Women attempt suicide more frequently than men.

This information is not meant to put women down. It is meant to help you open your eyes and see women for what they are: perfectly imperfect human beings. Flawed human beings who are no smarter, no better adjusted, no better put together, no more emotionally evolved than YOU!

Myth #2: Women are Complicated

This is one of the most prevalent myths about women – that they are complicated and difficult to understand. This isn't true; women are not complicated. While some women may be emotionally unpredictable, this doesn't make them complicated. The belief that women are complicated or difficult to understand keeps many men feeling frustrated and off-balance. Men often ask with bewilderment:

- Why did she do that?
- How come yesterday she was okay with that and today she blew up about the same thing?
- Why does she always change her mind?
- How come it is okay for her to do that, but if I do the same thing, there is all hell to pay?
- Why does she say she wants one thing (a "nice guy") and then does the opposite (date a "jerk")?

One reason women seem complicated to men is because the male brain and female brain are fundamentally different. In general, women have much more access to the right hemisphere of their brains than men do. The right side is the emotional side of the brain. Therefore, a woman's thinking and logic tends to be influenced more by feelings than a man's does. Since feelings change easily, so can a woman's logic. This doesn't make women complicated, it just means their logic might be a little more fluid than men's.

Female hormones also have a strong influence on the apparent *complexity* of some women. Sometimes, a woman's *unpredictability* is nothing more than the ebb and flow of female hormones – nothing complicated. Due to the monthly cycle of hormones, the average female brain can change physically up to 25% in a 30-day period (this is true)!

Another reason some women seem complicated is the result of mood disorders. BDs tend to be attracted to emotionally unstable women. This can include depressed women, bipolar women, sexual abuse survivors, and women with borderline personality disorder (BPD). These kinds of mood disorders can make some women appear complicated – especially when a man buys into the woman's reality. This will always lead to frustration, especially if a man believes there is a way to make sense of an emotionally unstable woman's changing moods or that these moods are a problem to be solved.

Here is the one thing I claim to know about women: *By nature, they tend to be security-seeking creatures.* Once I came to understand this, women became pretty simple and predictable to me. I've listened to women for over 30 years as a marriage counselor. Over and over again, women tell me their biggest complaint about their man is that they can't trust him or depend on him. Due to a deep emotional and physical need for security, trust means everything to a woman. Consequently, I regularly tell men that if a woman is acting in a way that he doesn't understand, her sense of security has probably been threatened.

So, instead of trying to figure a woman out, take her as she is at face value. *Set the tone, take the lead* (more about this in later chapters) and let her follow. When you try to figure a woman out and try to please her, you are doing the opposite of what will make her feel secure. A woman's security will come from you having a plan and being consistent and dependable. When she starts getting a little weird on you, step back and ask yourself, "How do I need to lovingly detach or set the tone in a more positive direction?"

Don't climb on her emotional roller coaster – she doesn't want you there. She wants to know that one of you still has their feet on the ground. Following her emotional lead only makes matters worse (review the previous chapter on how to calm and soothe yourself when a woman is acting like the weather).

Myth #3: Women are Naturally Good at Relationships

Most messages about relationships in our society are presented from a female point of view and aimed at a female audience. Oprah, Dr. Phil, and most books and magazines about relationships are directed at women. While women generally seem to be voracious consumers of this information, it doesn't mean that they are intrinsically good at relationships.

It is foolish to believe that just because a person has breasts and watches Oprah, she is good at relationships. Sure, many women spend a lot of time talking about relationships. But talking about relationships doesn't make one good at getting along with people any more than rehashing baseball statistics makes one good at hitting a major-league curveball. Ask yourself, if women are so good at relationships:

- Why do they have to buy so many books and magazines about a subject they are supposedly experts in?
- Why after watching so much Oprah and Dr. Phil do so many women still have difficulty taking charge of their own lives (why does Dr. Phil have to keep asking, "How's that working for you?")?
- Why do women pick bad men (and stay with them)?
- Why do women have problems getting along with each other?

It is important to smash this myth about women. In general, women don't want to be in charge of the relationship. When a man lets the woman set the tone of a relationship, he is doing the exact opposite of what will make her feel secure. Women consistently tell me that they want a man who will set the tone and take the lead – and not just in deciding where to go for dinner, but in the relationship as a whole. A woman shouldn't have to figure out where to go on a first date. A woman shouldn't have to pin a man down to get him to talk about relationship issues. A woman shouldn't have to drag a man into couples counseling.

Guys, it is your job to pay attention to what is going on in the relationship. Don't put this burden on the woman. When men force women to be the tenders of the relationship, it forces them to become controlling and/or nagging. That's not loving. Step up. Set the tone. Take the lead. Be honest, transparent, and revealing. Communicate. Deal with problems head on.

Myth #4: Women Expect Perfection from Men

BDs assume that women expect perfection when it comes to men. I frequently hear these men assert that the reason they don't have a girlfriend is that women only want tall, good looking, rich guys with power. This is an SLB that makes a good woman seem unattainable to the average guy. Think about it: If a woman feels flawed (most do), she won't be looking for a guy who seems more put together than she is. That would make her feel even more inadequate.

Women are a lot more forgiving and accepting than most men believe. Your shortcomings can often be assets if you accept them without judgment (i.e., shyness, anxiety, inexperience). Not every woman on the planet shares your negative view of these traits. It is your rough edges that make you interesting.

A healthy woman wants a guy who is real, honest, and confident in himself – not a perfect guy. Women consistently tell me they don't care that much what a man looks like or how much money he makes. What do women tell me they want? A man who is fun to be with, who will set the tone, and whom they can trust.

Myth #5: Friends to Lovers

Since most bad daters don't believe a woman whom they desire would desire them just the way they are, they often try and become a woman's "friend." These men tend to develop friendships with women hoping they will turn romantic in time. This is a bad dating strategy. And, it's terrible foreplay. The hope of a friendship turning into a sexual relationship almost never works. Once a woman sees a guy as "just a friend," this rarely changes. This is a significant way that women are different from men.

Women don't fuck a man they have gotten to know. They get to know a man they want to fuck.

One reason becoming friends rarely works is that the guy has repressed all of his sexual energy toward the woman because he thinks it will scare her off or ruin their friendship. While the woman may enjoy having the man be her *girlfriend with a penis,* it does nothing to turn her on or make her think about him in a *boyfriend* kind of way.

If you want to get a date, get a girlfriend or get laid, you have to get out of the *nursery.* This means you have to quit hanging around women with whom you're not having sex (this includes mothers, sisters, and female friends in general). These women are "safe" because they don't represent any kind of a sexual challenge. Spending too much time with women with whom you aren't having sex makes sexless relationships feel normal. If you want to find a girlfriend and/or sex partner, you have to hang around women with whom these are realistic possibilities.

When you spend too much non-sexual time with women, you quit seeing women as sexual objects (this is important even though we've been told we are bad men if we sexually objectify women). This stifles your healthy male sexuality and causes you to lose your sexual aura. Women observe this and never even think of you in sexual terms – "You're my friend, I couldn't have sex with YOU."

Myth #6: You Need a Woman to Complete You

The more power you give a woman to make you happy, the more power you give her to make you miserable. Women are the *icing,* not the *cake.* If you are looking for a woman to complete you – be the cake of your life – and give you meaning, purpose, and happiness, you will always be frustrated and resentful. If you take responsibility for creating an interesting and full life by embracing your passion, leaning into challenge, and having good relationships with men, then a good woman will be the icing that tops everything off.

Remember, women are people – just wounded creatures walking the planet. When you discover this secret and allow it to guide your life, you will be ahead of about 90 percent of the men out there. You will also be able to approach women with confidence. While women may look and, at times, think and act differently from you, they are still just people. They are not superior to you, they are not complicated, and they won't make your life complete.

But women can be fun, challenging, and stimulating if you see them clearly for who they are. If you want to be able to talk to them, date them, have sex with them, marry them – you have to blast the myths you have come to believe to be true. You'll benefit and so will the women you meet.

CHAPTER 8: BREAK YOUR ADDICTION TO SUPERFICIAL BEAUTY

Beauty fades, but mean, moody, and entitled last forever.

A common trait of bad daters is an obsession with *young* and/or *hot women*. While it is important for men to date women whom they find attractive, putting young and hot women on a pedestal is detrimental to both men and women.

While many dating books and seminars focus on picking up hot women, I believe this is misguided. These programs only perpetuate the cultural mythology around beautiful women. This keeps men feeling dependent and powerless around these women.

Here is the curious thing about the dating and seduction gurus who claim to teach men how to pick up hot and/or younger women – not one that I've come across actually spells out what the advantage is of getting a hot or beautiful woman. There is just the understood assumption that we all know why this is a good idea.

While having sex with a healthy, well-proportioned woman makes sense from an evolutionary point of view (it increases the odds of having healthy babies), an obsession with hot women is basically broadcasting a man's low sense of self. Only a man with extremely low self-esteem would believe that having a young, hot, or beautiful woman would somehow give him worth, meaning, and value.

I've listened to countless men who are socially awkward, underachieving, and out of shape, unequivocally state that unless they can date a 10, they don't want to date at all. One of my clients told me he was "lowering his standards by dating women close to his own age (this was the result of him being so intimidated by the young, attractive women he desired, that he could never get up the nerve to approach any of them).

This is like stating, "Unless I can drive a Bentley, I won't drive at all." On the surface it sounds juvenile, shallow, and superficial. But on a deeper level it makes sense.

We have talked about how much anxiety most BDs have around interacting with women (any women). They find all kinds of creative ways to keep their anxiety in check. One of the most effective is to become obsessed with dating young and attractive women. Since most BDs really believe that such women would never give them the time of day, they are safe. By setting unrealistic standards, they can justify not dating at all. This keeps them safe.

Just for the record, I make a distinction between *hot* women and women with natural beauty. My definition of a *hot* woman is "a woman who needs to be noticed and validated for her physical appearance." Because of this need, they dress provocatively, augment their bodies, and act in highly sensual ways. This isn't the same as having natural attractiveness or wanting to look nice.

I also want to be clear. I believe men should date women to whom they are attracted. But I also believe that it is good practice to talk to all women. Waiting until you see a woman to whom you are physically attracted before you practice your interpersonal and social skills will only result in you doing nothing.

There are a lot of really great women out there who aren't 20 years younger than you, who don't have big boobs, and who don't spend thousands of dollars on clothes, cosmetics, and plastic surgery. Get to know some of these women. If you're holding out for the 10s, you're going to miss out on a lot of really cool chicks!

I want you to imagine something. Let's say you are walking through your local mall and you spot a famous celebrity (it could happen). Let's say you spot LeBron James, or George Clooney, or Jay-Z.

How likely would you be to approach such a celebrity and start a conversation? Would you walk up to them and just start chatting? Would you invite them out for drinks or dinner? If you are like most people, you would feel intimidated, you wouldn't want to intrude, and you wouldn't know what to say, so you would just gawk from a distance.

Let's take it a step further. What if one of these celebrities actually approached you and invited you to hang out with him? He invited you to go to Cannes with him, to ride in his private jet, to hang out in his mansion. How comfortable would you be setting the tone in this kind of relationship? How much time would you spend waiting for the other shoe to fall and for him to drop you as a buddy and take up with some other celebrity?

Here's the analogy: Most BDs turn young and/or attractive women into *sexual celebrities*. They put beautiful women up on a pedestal and act just like they would with a real celebrity. They admire but don't approach. If they approach, they do it awkwardly. If by some fluke, they get into a relationship with a woman they see as a sexual celebrity, they are passive and pleasing. They live in fear waiting for the day she finds a better man.

Now tell me why you think it's a great idea to pursue young, hot or beautiful women? Statistically, you are more likely to have success dating and creating a healthy, satisfying long-term relationship if you date close to your own age and appearance level. If you are a five or six, don't fantasize about or pursue 10s. Don't date down, but don't chase beauty.

Human attraction is based on so many more things than just physical features. Of course, finding someone you are physically attracted to is a good start. A woman's physical features get your attention and motivate you to reach out and connect. But if you only approach or talk to hot women, or if physical appearance is your only reason for being with a woman, you are not only broadcasting your immaturity, but you are also in for a boatload of relationship problems.

You are an evolving, complex, and interesting person. I expect that you would want a woman to be attracted to you for a multitude of good reasons, not just one superficial feature that you have little control over. A mature man is naturally attracted to a woman based on a number of characteristics, not just what is visible to the eye.

Is she:

- Happy?
- Generous?

- Affectionate?
- Smart?
- Fun?
- Playful?
- Disciplined?
- Passionate?
- Honest?
- Mature?

Does she:

- Have a good sense of humor?
- Get along with people?
- Treat people with compassion **and respect?**
- Communicate well?
- Handle her money with discipline?
- Take good care of herself?
- Like sex?
- Work through problems?
- Own her shit?

I think you get it.

Approach Vs. Attraction

Here is the question I am most frequently asked in my *Dating Essentials for Men* programs:

"What do I do when I see a woman I like?"

My initial response is typically, "**What do** you mean you like her? You don't even know her! How could you **know** you like her?"

Then the ensuing conversation goes something like this:

"You know, she's hot. I like how **she looks.** I'm attracted to her."

"Liking someone and being physically attracted to someone are two completely different things. I've found it helpful not to confuse them."

"Okay, I think she's attractive. **How do** I get her attention without coming off like a creep or looking like **I'm hitting on her?"**

"You *are* hitting on her! Why do you think that makes you a creep?"

"Well, I just want to get to know her, find out if she's a cool chick."

"Why do you want to get to know her? Because you like her tits? Her ass? The truth is, you hope that maybe you'll get to see her naked someday. That is why you want to talk to her. And guess what, she knows that."

"No, really, she just seems cool. I just want to talk to her."

"Would you think the same way if she were 50 pounds overweight or twice your age?"

"I don't understand."

"Your male brain is sexually objectifying this particular woman based on a few physical traits, and you believe that because she turns you on, she might make a good girlfriend. Because you have already put her up on a pedestal, you now have to figure out how to get her to notice you, be interested in you, give you her number, go on a date with you, have sex with you, and keep wanting to hang out with you over time. That sounds like a hell of a lot of work to me. And you are basing all of this on a few physical traits. No matter what your male brain is telling you about what she could do for you, it's a lie. Just remember this: beautiful fades, but moody, mean, and entitled are forever."

"You mean I shouldn't talk to her?"

"I mean, finding someone physically attractive is the worst reason imaginable for walking across a room and starting a conversation with a complete stranger. Maybe it would be easier to start paying attention to the women who are already drawn to you and giving you signals of their interest. Maybe you would save yourself boatloads of hard work and a possible lifetime of grief by choosing this kind of woman rather than chasing after unicorns who don't know you exist and couldn't care less."

"But I want a hot girlfriend."

"I know; everyone does."

Why *Dating Essentials for Men* is Different

A primary goal of *Dating Essentials for Men* is to help men change their thinking from *approach to attraction*.

I'm not a fan of approach – and especially *pickup* – for a number of reasons.

Approach is always based on attachment to outcome.

When you approach, you are trying to make something happen. By nature, approach (and especially pickup) is always based on attachment to a specific outcome. You desire a specific woman – usually based on her physical attributes – and you want her to desire you back (or least give you her number).

Approach tends to be adolescent in nature (even when we try to convince ourselves it isn't).

The ego-based attachment behind approach is shallow: you typically want to engage with a woman for one primary reason – her looks. While it is normal to be attracted to young and/or attractive women, using a woman's physical appearance as your primary reason for interacting with her is pretty one-dimensional and adolescent. It is every bit as shallow as women chasing after men solely for their money.

Approach gives a woman all the power – it makes you the Beta and her the Alpha.

You have put a woman you are attracted to up on a pedestal, and now she is the "decider" (especially if she is used to having lots of men put her up on a pedestal). This sets up a power differential that will never work in your favor. She gets to choose; you don't.

Approach creates a culture of entitlement in women.

Men's obsession with 10s has created a dynamic in our culture in which women have so much perceived power and very little accountability. We men have given physically attractive women all this power for absolutely nothing. We value them solely because they have the dumb luck of good genes or because they've spent a lot of money on makeup, hair, and clothes. What is their real value beyond all that? By approaching women purely because we find them attractive, we men have given these women license to be entitled brats. Then we turn around and resent them for all the power we have given them.

Approach is the result of male mythical thinking.

Approach is always a manifestation of your male mythological mind that creates a fantasy around what an attractive woman can do for you. Your mind assumes that because you like the way her legs, breasts, ass, and face look your life will somehow be better if she were your girlfriend or if she fucked you.

Approach creates a terrible foundation for an ongoing relationship.

Even if something comes from your approach, it establishes a bad pattern from then on. You will always be seeking this woman's approval, and you will probably put up with all kinds of crap because you don't want to lose her and you don't want to have to start the approach-dependent dating process all over again.

Shifting the Paradigm

Everything proves much easier if you practice the principles I teach in *Dating Essentials for Men* that make you naturally attractive to women.

Here is an important truth: *It is much easier to walk through open doors than to pound on closed doors.* Approach typically amounts to pounding on closed doors, trying to gain entry. Attraction allows you to choose from many open doors. Walking through open doors is a hell of a lot easier and more rewarding than pounding on closed ones.

When I do use the word *approach* in this book, it isn't in the typical, "you see a hot woman you are attracted to and you walk across a crowded room to try to start a conversation with her" kind of approach. When a woman is sending you signals of high interest (IOIs), by all means, approach her (we will talk more about this). Introduce yourself to her. Test for interest. Walk through the open door.

When you practice the principles I teach in DEFM, and when you live an attractive lifestyle, you will begin to see women sending you all kinds of signals of interest. Some will be subtle, and some will be a grab-you-by-the-balls-and-demand-that-you-fuck-her-now signal of interest (believe me, it happens).

When a woman is sending you signals of interest – smiling at you, holding eye contact, repeatedly walking in front of you, laughing at your jokes, touching your arm, flirting, repeatedly looking your way, standing close to you, positioning her body directly in your line of sight, leaning forward and flashing some cleavage – by all means, approach! But remember, you are the decider.

Over the last several years, I've had no shortage of great women expressing high interest in me. I've had no shortage of loving relationships.

I've had no shortage of amazing sex with countless fun, sexy women. Since I started living and practicing the principles of attraction that I teach in *Dating Essentials for Men*, I have often asked myself, "What planet have I landed on?"

When I shifted from an approach-based, *seduction* mentality, women started propositioning me, getting naked on first dates, and calling me at 11:00 PM for hook-ups. I had to start deleting women's names and numbers from my cell phone every few months because I had so many and couldn't remember who they all were.

I have never pursued young or attractive women, but the majority of women who express high interest in me are typically many years younger than me and very attractive (amazing how many of them were cheerleaders in high school – I never could have dated a cheerleader when I was in high school). I didn't chase these women; they came to me.

I am not making any of this up, and I would not have believed it myself before I discovered what I am teaching you here. When you practice what I teach in *Dating Essentials for Men*, you don't have to chase hot women. Instead, you will naturally attract an unimaginable number of amazing women into your life.

Here is a principle I borrowed from David Deida, the author of *The Way of The Superior Man* that has served me well: "Choose a woman who chooses you."

Wouldn't you rather choose from many great women who are already expressing high interest in you, rather than spend your time, money, and energy knocking on closed doors? When you choose a woman who has chosen you, you get to be the decider. You get to be the Alpha. You get to be the man among men.

Let go of the games, the banter, the tricks, the seduction, the buying women drinks, the volunteering to help their sisters move, the pounding on closed doors. Practice what I am teaching you in this book and learn how to create the kind of attraction that brings women to you. Then, just walk through the open door (it really is that easy). You will wonder what planet you've landed on.

How do you create that lifestyle that naturally attracts women? Keep reading.

CHAPTER 9: CREATE A LIFESTYLE THAT ATTRACTS WOMEN NATURALLY

A great woman is the icing, not the cake.

When I began dating in my late 40s after 25 years of marriage, I had no real idea how to get started. One of the first things I did was sign up for an online dating site. As I began reading the profiles of the women, I had a "holy shit" experience. It seemed like every woman online was living an amazing life. They all skied (downhill, cross country, water), sailed, hiked, danced, ran marathons, rollerbladed, ran their own companies, drank great wine, and traveled the world. They all wanted a man who could match their lifestyles and spark instant chemistry – "Wow!"

I quickly realized that these profiles were the result of women going a little overboard to make a good impression. There just weren't enough hours in the day for these superwomen to be doing all the things they claimed to do – but it still got my attention. Online dating was a wakeup call.

Creating my own profile was a revealing process. Since adolescence, I had believed that being a *great guy* would be sufficient to get a woman to notice me and want to go out with me. Unfortunately, being a Nice Guy only attracted women with problems that needed fixing. The process of writing my online profile illuminated the reality that I didn't have much of a life. It hit me that being a no-life Nice Guy wasn't going to attract the kind of woman I wanted. *In order to naturally attract amazing women to me, I had to create an amazing life.*

It wasn't that I thought I had to spice up my life just to attract a woman. I realized I needed to create a more interesting life FOR ME! So, I set out to create a passionate, active, fulfilled, interesting, growing, and happy life. I was right. The better my life has become, the better the women have become. And, the better my life has become, the less I've had to work at attracting the kind of women I want.

Bringing Something to the Table

People get into relationships because there is some payoff. Think about this; you want a relationship (or sex) with a woman who brings something to the table. What if a woman sat home all day, talking on the phone, eating Ben & Jerry's, and watching reruns of the *Kardashians*? Would you find that interesting or attractive? Would you think to yourself, "Man, that's the ideal woman for me"?

No! You want a woman who has something going on! Every man is attracted to different things in a woman, but every guy wants a woman who adds some value to his life. Ideally, you are looking for a smart, funny, flexible, passionate, and responsible woman who has a few friends, takes good care of herself and thinks you're great. It helps if she reads a book every now and then, has some understanding of current events, pays her bills on time, and knows her way around the gym. Bottom line, you want an interesting and evolving human being.

A woman like this is going to expect similar things from you. Fair enough? To get what you want in love and sex, you have to take stock of your life. Just being nice, in your head, codependent, or good at World of Warcraft isn't enough to attract a woman's attention and keep her interested.

This chapter will help you evaluate what changes you need to make in order to naturally attract a Really Great Woman. While you are doing this, you have to continue challenging your old SLBs that have convinced you that an RGW can't love you just as you are. This isn't a contradiction.

You have to work at being the kind of man a woman would want AND accept yourself just as you are.

Bad daters often create a paradox for themselves. Because of their self-limiting beliefs, they don't think an RGW would want them due to all of their perceived faults and flaws. Yet, they often won't do anything to improve themselves or address their perceived weaknesses. These men will often obsess about being overweight, bald, disorganized, uninteresting, or bad with money. They use these SLBs to justify not interacting with women, yet won't take proactive measures to do what they can to improve themselves.

Women probably won't reject you for all the reasons you have convinced yourself they will, yet they do expect you to bring something to the table. This isn't a contradiction, it is a truth that successful daters understand. Most women don't care if you are bald or carrying a few extra pounds, but they expect you to make the best of what you've got! If this makes sense to you, you are on your way to a really great life with tons of potential for attracting some really great women!

The Currency of Attraction

David DeAngelo (Eben Pagan), the creator of *Double Your Dating* makes the assertion that "attraction is not a choice." I agree with this. People are attracted to one another for all kinds of unconscious reasons that often make very little sense and, at times, defy logic and rationality. Trying to predict what one person will be attracted to in another person is futile and frustrating. Don't try.

So, what is the currency of attraction? What is there about you and your life that women might find interesting? While I won't assert that any one thing will attract women, a good rule of thumb is to work on developing all the traits you would like your ideal partner to possess. If you want a self-confident woman who takes good care of herself, develop those traits in yourself. If you want an honest woman, become an honest man. If you want a passionate, expressive woman, become that yourself.

If you are 40-pounds overweight, can't make eye contact with women, and spend most of your free time at home surfing the internet, don't expect attractive, active women to be attracted to you. *Become what you want to attract.* That's the way it works.

Understand What Women Want

Women are both security seeking creatures and sensual creatures. Most men don't understand the significance of these two realities. Men tend to approach the world analytically – as a problem to be solved. The biggest mistake BDs make is assuming women are just like them.

If you haven't noticed, women tend to be highly influenced by their feelings. This is because the female brain is wired to experience life through all five senses (as opposed to the one or two senses the male brain uses).

For example, being *nice* doesn't turn women on. Even when they proclaim they want to find a *nice guy,* nice doesn't make women feel secure and doesn't activate their senses in a powerful way. They may think they want a nice guy, but biology prevents them from actually being attracted to a passively pleasing man. Successful daters understand this reality and take advantage of it.

If you keep these two facts in mind – women are security seeking creatures and sensual creatures – then you will better understand what you have to bring to the dating table to naturally attract the kind of women you want. You may interpret this to mean that in order to appeal to a woman, you have to be rich, spend a lot of money, and give her nice things. This is typical BD thinking, and it's wrong.

As security seeking creatures and sensual creatures, women are attracted to what makes them feel good and gives them a sense of well-being. If you take advantage of this reality, you will never lack for dates and you will greatly increase the odds of finding a Really Great Woman!

As a marriage therapist, I've been listening to women tell me what they want (and don't want) from men for over 30 years. I've taken these principles and tested them with women I've dated. I've taken polls from random women all over the world. Here is what I've found over and over again from women of all ages and backgrounds.

A woman wants:

- A man she can trust.
- A man who makes her feel secure.
- A man who can set the tone and take the lead.
- A man who has passion.

- A man who can make her laugh.
- An intelligent man (not just analytical).
- A man who is generous and compassionate.
- A man who is socially aware.
- A man who has a healthy sense of self.
- A man who takes good care of himself.
- A man who is honest and transparent.
- A man who can reveal what he is thinking and feeling.
- A man who has integrity.
- A man who can admit fault and laugh at himself.
- A man who embraces his masculinity.
- A man who has good guy friends.
- A man who is comfortable with his sexuality.

Women find these traits attractive because they make them *feel secure and good*. Notice that none of these traits have anything to do with being tall, good looking, or rich. Most women aren't looking for the perfect man. They're looking for a man who understands their need to feel safe and their need for beauty, passion and sensuality.

Here is a true story: A woman emailed me after listening to one of my podcasts during which I talk about men bringing the following traits to their relationship: consciousness, honesty, transparency, and leadership (setting the tone and taking the lead). She asked me if men really could show up and consistently manifest these four traits. When I assured her that a mature man can, here is what she wrote in response:

"I honestly think you should begin a dating service for the guys who do your course. They would seriously be inundated with options. A guy who is focused on being conscious, honest, transparent and taking the lead??!? I mean, hello. Women would go nuts. I talked about these four principles with a good woman friend of mine today and her entire body lit up! It's nuts."

Look over these traits I've listed above. Ask yourself if there are any that you can't realistically develop with just a little introspection and effort. This is what I mean about challenging your SLBs AND putting some effort into what you have to offer to a potential RGW.

Challenge Your SLBs

Warning! The following information might initially feel overwhelming. It will probably trigger your SLBs that you have to get it all together *before* you can attract the kind of women you want. Don't listen to these voices. They are distorted.

Your SLBs and board of directors don't want you to get a life and attract lots of really great women. A part of your mind wants you to feel defeated and keep doing what you've been doing. It is familiar territory. It is low anxiety. Challenging yourself to create a full life will take you into new, unknown, and frightening places. It will trigger anxiety and fear.

Replace those old, familiar SLBs with new beliefs that proclaim you don't have to be perfect. You can get out there *and* date *while* you are working on yourself. Tell yourself that you don't have to do everything at once, you can handle change, you can handle happiness, and you can handle having an RGW (or several Really Great Women) in your life.

As we have talked about in previous chapters, *what you think is what you will be and what you will attract.* How many women will you attract by telling yourself that you are worthless? If you are going to tell yourself something, why not something positive? Why would a woman be attracted to a guy who doesn't think very highly of himself?

How much sense does it make to walk around telling yourself, "I'm boring, unattractive, and have no life"? What woman would ever give you a second look when you are projecting this attitude through your behavior and body language? Why not walk around telling yourself, "I'm interesting, articulate and any woman would be lucky to have me!"? If you have to pick one, why would you be demeaning to yourself? Why not choose the loving, affirming message?

Don't expect a really great woman to think more highly of you than you do yourself. Creating a great life requires you to observe and challenge your old SLBs every day. You don't have to do it perfectly or do it all now. You'll spend the rest of your life clearing out the old baggage and discovering how great you really are. Give all the great women out there a chance to find out too!

Make a Great Cake

As I shared in Chapter 7, it is a myth to believe that a woman can complete you in any way. If you are looking for a woman to fill you up or compensate for anything that is missing in your life, you will never feel whole or happy. A woman can't be the center of your life. You have to make a great cake of a life and only then can a woman be the icing on top.

Many BDs often feel victimized by a less than satisfying life, yet most relationship-challenged men rarely take stock of what kind of life they want to live and actively go after it. *The core premise of Dating Essentials for Men is that you can let go of SLBs and create a fantastic, fulfilling life.*

Following the principles in this book won't just help you get dates, it will help you create a really great life! Hopefully, you will keep growing, evolving, and challenging yourself until the day you die. This is the recipe for making a great cake. While it takes many ingredients to make a cake, and there are many different kinds of cake, I believe there are a few key ingredients that are essential in order for men to live a great life and attract great women. Again, you don't have to do these things perfectly, but working at them consistently and keeping them in balance is essential for great cake-making.

Key great cake ingredients:

Key Ingredient #1: Passion

The first of the key ingredients for a great cake is pursuing your passions in life. This is essential. The only way to have a full life is to pursue your passions through work, hobby, and recreation. This doesn't mean just working a lot. It means working and playing at what makes you completely happy and fulfilled.

Masculinity is defined by this passion. I've worked with many men who have never discovered or pursued their passions or who have sacrificed them to focus on taking care of the needs of other people. I made the latter mistake for the first 25 years of my adult life. Ironically it cost me not only my relationships, but my own life energy.

As a therapist, I've worked with hundreds of couples. In several instances, the woman insisted that she should be her man's number one priority. This is a recipe for disaster. A man must make his passion his number one priority. By doing so, he gives his woman (or women) something to be attracted to. Once he **makes** something else his number one priority, he loses the masculinity **energy** that naturally attracts feminine energy.

Passion rule of thumb #1: *Stop doing anything you aren't doing with passion and start doing everything you do with passion.* Shave with passion. Do the dishes with passion. Drive **with** passion. Balance your checkbook with passion. Interact with women **with** passion. Fuck with passion.

Passion rule of thumb #2: *Turn every "oh no I have to," into an "oh boy I get to!"* Try it, you will be amazed at how this little rule will lighten your load and make you more attractive to **all** things feminine.

Key Ingredient #2: Guy Friends

Another key ingredient for creating **a** great life is having good guy friends. I discovered this during my **second** marriage. I realized at one point that my whole life revolved around **my** wife and kids. I had no male friends. This was the first thing I decided **to** work on when I began recovering from the Nice Guy Syndrome.

I noticed a significant improvement in the quality of my relationship with my wife when I began building **these** relationships with men. She would even comment on how much **more** attracted she was to me when I spent time with men. As a single man, I've had women quiz me on a first date about my guy friends because they **know** how vital it is to having a healthy relationship.

Having good buddies is the foundation of your intimate relationships. A good relationship with a woman can **only** be built on this foundation. Without the foundation of guy friends, **you'll** become needy and codependent in your relationship with a **woman.** A woman can't meet all of your relationship needs. When you **have** good relationships with men, you won't put the pressure on a woman **to** fill you up. Your guy friends will already be doing this for you. Plus, **hanging** out with men raises your testosterone level and that's a good thing.

I know that these days you often **hear** and read about partners being each other's *best friend.* This sounds **great,** but it is severely misguided. I don't believe a person of the opposite **sex** can truly be a best friend. When couples come to me for marriage counseling, I often tell them during the first session that one of the best things they can for their marriage is have good same-sex friends. Men need the masculine connection and women need the feminine connection. No matter how good a friend a member of the opposite sex may be, they can't connect with you or understand you in the way a friend of the same sex can.

Say for example your girlfriend is your *best friend*. What if you have a fight with her? Or what if you need to talk about her to a non-biased person? Who are you going to talk to? If your partner is your best friend, you're in trouble. Good relationships need same-sex best friends to help them through challenging times. Your partner can't do this double duty for you and you can't do it for her either!

Building relationships with men is a lifelong proposition. I have found that it is much easier to meet women and create relationships with the opposite sex than it is to meet men and form close relationships. I have also found that as men's lives change (marriage, divorce, children, work, moves), so do their friendships. This means that you have to keep working to make new guy friends while staying in touch with the ones you have, even when life circumstances change. It takes ongoing effort, but it's worth it.

Key Ingredient #3: Regular, Strenuous Exercise

Another essential ingredient for a great life is physical fitness that results from regular exercise. I'm talking about four to five days a week of strenuous exercise – sweat pouring off your forehead. It doesn't matter what you do, but you have to exert yourself on a daily basis. You can run, bike, lift weights, shoot hoops, practice yoga, play tennis – whatever you enjoy – but it has to be regular and it has to be strenuous.

There are several benefits to regular exercise. The first is obvious – it keeps you in shape. Men who don't maintain good physical condition suffer the consequences. A lack of exercise leads to health issues like heart disease and diabetes. Not to mention that exercising helps mood and sleep. Of course, there is also a psychological benefit to exercise. You'll be happy with how you look when you are in shape. If you want a great life, you have to lose your gut and build up your body. As with everything else in life, this requires consistency over time.

Key Ingredient #4: Lean Into Challenge

There is at least one more major benefit to regular strenuous exercise. When you are exercising on a regular basis, the same discipline that gets you into the gym every day becomes evident in every other area of your life. You will find that you become more disciplined with your work, with your home, and your life in general. All of these things make you feel better and, thus, make you more attractive.

Many of the men with whom I work tend to regularly choose comfort over challenge. This is why they often procrastinate, become easily frustrated, do the easy thing rather than the hard thing, fail to live up to their potential, lack discipline, and avoid. It is why they turn to addictions like food, alcohol, and porn. It is why they seek a woman to fill them up.

As long as you are seeking comfort in life, you will never find it. Comfort never satisfies. Seeking comfort will never take you far in life, nor will it make you very attractive. It is only through leaning into challenge that you grow, feel complete, and look attractive to the opposite sex. This is what the discipline of regular, strenuous exercise can do for you.

Additional ingredients for a great cake of a life include; *spiritual practices* (meditation, therapy, support groups, reading uplifting and positive books, faith, praying, etc.), and *giving your gift to the world* (give without expectation, walk the planet with integrity, do things for people that they can't do for themselves, smile).

In order to bake a great cake of a life:

- You have to make your life passion your number one priority.
- You have to develop and maintain good friendships with men.
- You have to engage in strenuous exercise on a daily basis.
- You have to lean into challenge on a daily basis.
- You have to develop and maintain a spiritual practice.
- You have to give your gift to the world.

If you leave out any of these ingredients or let them get out of balance, you will unconsciously seek something else to fill the void. These fillers – like food, alcohol, drugs, porn, a woman, or excessive work – will never complete you. Like emotional junk food, they will merely perpetuate the empty feeling you are hoping they will satisfy.

Here are some additional ingredients to help create your great cake of a life – the kind of life that will satisfy you and make you attractive to women (we will explore many of these in upcoming chapters):

- Get organized.
- Keep your car and house clean.
- Pay attention to personal grooming.
- Create a beautiful space around you (home/office).
- Learn to dance.
- Have regular hobbies.
- Do it now – eliminate the stress of having things hanging over you.
- Get out of debt, save.
- Make your bed, do your dishes, hang up your clothes, and clean your bathroom – every day.
- Limit television and internet surfing.
- Take classes.

Never Quit Making Your Great Cake

So, you've worked hard to create a great life, one that is fulfilling to you and one that is attractive to women. Let's say you meet someone who appears to have the potential to be a Really Great Woman and you start spending time together. This is natural in a new relationship. You both want to spend as much time together as possible.

You go on dates, hang out, watch television together, chat on the phone, take trips. Eventually, you might move in together and share household chores and projects. You believe you have found the woman you have been looking for, and you want to spend as much time with her as you can.

Unfortunately, this is the beginning of the end! Here is why: When you first meet a woman who has the potential to be your RGW, you are probably both living lives that are fulfilling and interesting. This is what makes you attracted to each other. But, as you both begin spending more time together, you have less time to engage in the things you were both doing before you met.

Some couples start spending so much time together that they completely let go of everything they were doing when they first met. This is called *fusion*. *Fusion is where both people lose themselves as a result of the relationship.* There are at least two major problems when people fuse.

The first problem that fusion creates is that *neither is the same person that the other was originally attracted to.* Do you ever wonder how you could initially find someone so interesting, but the more time you spend with her, the less interested you are in being with her? One reason is that she has changed. The very act of spending time together has caused both of you to sacrifice the lifestyle that once made you interesting to each other. She's not the same person you were originally attracted to.

The second problem is that *as you both give up important things in your lives, you both expect the other person to fill the void.* This is a heavy burden to place on any one person. It creates neediness and dependency, as well as resentment and boredom. When you fail to fill each other up, you blame each other. Then, you both attempt to get the other person to change and become something that will fill the inner void you are both experiencing.

This is why it is essential to hold onto your full life and practice differentiation, even after you move into an intimate relationship. *Differentiation is the ability to hold on to yourself when there is pressure to fuse and lose yourself to another.* Differentiation is essential for personal happiness and relationship health.

So, when you find a Really Great Woman and all you can think about is being with her every moment, remember what got you there. Hold onto yourself. Stay differentiated – keep making the cake. Pursue your passion. Keep your guy friends. Stay faithful at the gym. Keep leaning into challenge. Maintain your spiritual practice. Keep giving your gift to the world.

There will still be time for you and your woman to enjoy each other. Maintain balance and stay differentiated. Remember, she's the icing, not the cake.

CHAPTER 10: ACTIVATE WOMEN'S BASIC BIOLOGICAL URGES

I'm useless without my mojo. – Austin Powers

In the 1999 classic, Austin Powers, The Spy Who Shagged Me, Dr. Evil travels back to 1969 in a "time machine" to steal Austin Powers' "mojo." As soon as Dr. Evil drinks his nemesis's "life force," he becomes irresistible to Frau Frisian. The effect on Austin Powers, International Man of Mystery, is catastrophic.

The irrepressible 60s swinger becomes anxious, nervous, self-conscious, and impotent. He is unable to follow through on an opportunity to have his way with Felicity Shagwell. As a result, Felicity blames herself for not being adequately attractive. Austin arrives at the painful conclusion, "I'm useless without my mojo."

Not having *mojo* is a major problem for most bad daters. A lack of mojo ("libido, vitality, life force" – according to Dr. Evil) is probably a fundamental reason you have experienced frustration and rejection with women.

Mojo empowers you to interact with women confidently. It is what causes women to notice you and want you. It is what gives you the backbone to walk away from the wrong woman. It is what makes you think positively and abundantly.

This chapter will show you how to claim your mojo. It will reveal the secret for meeting women with optimal confidence and minimal anxiety. This chapter isn't for the faint of heart. It will challenge everything you have ever believed about how you should interact with women. It will force you take a long hard look at some of your debilitating, yet socially sanctioned SLBs. What I am going to say might frighten you, but if you are ready to get what you want in love and sex then it is time to claim your mojo and get busy!

The Lie of Niceness

The problem most BDs have is that they either don't interact with women at all, or if they do, they engage with them "nicely."

Think back to junior high or middle school. This is the age when you began to really notice girls. These suddenly interesting creatures were not only developing physically, they also seemed more socially interesting than most of your guy friends. About a year or two after the girls started developing, so did you. All of a sudden, your brain and testicles started telling you that it might be a good idea to get the attention of one of these sexy creatures.

Unfortunately, you might not have had the greatest social skills. You were awkward. You probably weren't great looking, rich, or the quarter-back of the football team. Your reach exceeded your grasp. So, you concluded that you needed some kind of plan to stand out from the crowd of pimply awkward adolescent boys who all had the same goal as you (and also didn't have a clue).

It was probably around this time that you came up with a strategy for making you different from the other guys. You would be *nice.* Your 14-year-old mind told you that this was probably your best approach for winning a girl's affection. You might have also developed a secondary strategy – homing in on the girls who were the most insecure. You may have unconsciously reasoned that a diamond in the rough wouldn't have expectations as high as the more desirable girls.

Unfortunately, these strategies didn't work then and they don't work now, that's because there are a few major problems with the "nice" strategy:

Being nice to a woman is an overt attempt to win her approval. Seeking approval actually ratchets up your anxiety level. If you don't care what a woman thinks about you, you can interact with her with a calm detachment that projects confidence. Caring too much about what a woman thinks makes you timid, anxious, and fearful. As a result, either you don't engage at all, or you do so with great reserve.

Being nice makes you appear lower in status than the woman with whom you are interacting. People usually only suck up to those who are greater in status (at least perceived). When you are being overly polite, gracious, giving, solicitous, and passively pleasing with a woman, she will perceive you to be of lower status.

Being nice does absolutely nothing to turn a woman on. I know the opposite is true for you. When a woman is nice to you, it gets your attention and gets you fantasizing about her. But for women, it just makes you look like a *friend*. A woman may want to be attracted to a nice guy, but biology won't allow it. Being nice puts a cork in her biologically programmed juices, it will kill any spark of attraction she might have originally had for you.

Being nice creates a terrible foundation for any ongoing relationship. Once you start trying to win a woman's approval by being nice, the pattern never ends. Even if you end up in a relationship with a woman, you have created a dynamic of trying to please her and make her happy (while trying to keep her from leaving you). This is a recipe for disaster in relationships (Trust me, I've done it a few times and watched it thousands of times).

Niceness will do nothing more than send you straight to the *friend zone*. She might take advantage of your willingness to listen for hours. She might tell you about the problems she is having with the jerk she is dating. She might ask you to help her sister move. But she will never want to have sex with you – you are her "friend."

Why You Want a Woman

Right now you are probably thinking, "Don't be nice? Are you suggesting I become a jerk?" I know, you've been trying to be different from the jerks for all these years. Most BDs tend to think in black and white, so becoming a jerk might seem like the only alternative to being nice, but there is another, much more effective alternative.

Ask yourself this question: What is the primary reason for interacting with a woman you find attractive?

- So you can listen to her talk about her problems?
- So you can buy her drinks?
- So you can spend your hard-earned money paying off her bills?

No! You approach a woman you are attracted to for one primary reason – SEX! This is the reason you found girls interesting at 14 and it is the reason you find women interesting now. I know this truth just triggered some huge SLBs for you:

- But that would make me a bad man.
- Turning women into sex objects is demeaning.
- Women will think I'm a jerk if they know I want to have sex with them.

God gave women breasts so you would find them interesting enough to talk to them. Of course, you are evolved enough to not just see women as sex objects, but it is still the primary reason for your initial desire to interact with them – and they know this.

Mother Nature made you want to put your penis in vaginas because it is the most effective way to keep the human race in existence. (Have you ever pondered the fact that every one of your ancestors had sex?) Who are you to argue with Mother Nature? You won't win that argument. *It is evolutionary sin to repress your God-given sexual interest in women.*

If you believe your sex drive makes you a bad man, you're believing a lie. It is also a lie that women will think you are bad if you want to have sex with them. In fact, the opposite is true. Felicity Shagwell felt worthless and rejected when Austin couldn't get it up for her, remember?

Confidence – The Number One Aphrodisiac

I suggest that you read the following sentence several times until it really sinks in: *When you approach a woman with confidence, she experiences the exact same chemical reaction in her brain (the release of dopamine and norepinephrine) that you would experience if she lifted up her shirt and showed you her breasts.*

You can't help what happens in your brain and she can't help what happens in hers. Mother Nature has programmed these reactions into both of you. Since women are security seeking creatures, confidence, status, power, and authority all activate their biologically programmed security meters.

The biggest drawback for most BDs is not that they aren't attractive enough, smart enough, or successful enough – it is that they project a lack of confidence.

Imagine this: You are walking through the mall and happen to notice an attractive woman walking toward you. You unconsciously check her out. All of a sudden, she looks your way. She sees you looking at her. What do you instinctively do? If you are like the majority of men, you look away. You think you've been caught. You're sure she'll know that you were looking at her and think you're a jerk. What message does your looking away project? Confidence or passivity, dominance or submission, status or subservience?

Confident men will hold the woman's gaze and smile confidently. The woman gives either a high interest or low interest response. Regardless of whether or not she is attracted to the man, she will perceive him as confident and assured. She'll feel a little buzz. She'll walk with a skip in her step and might not even realize why. By looking away, you communicate that you are submissive, intimidated, and unsure of yourself. It isn't what you meant to communicate, but unfortunately, this is how it will be interpreted. These are the type of inadvertent signals most BDs send to women.

The sad thing is, you probably looked away because your SLBs told you that a woman will think you are bad if she catches you checking her out. This is a lie. A woman will think you have status and power if you are checking her out (unless you are flat out staring at her and undressing her with your eyes – this is creepy). Unless you are dressed like a street person, the only clue a woman has to your status is how you carry yourself and how you hold her gaze.

SLBs and Sex

Most BDs have extreme shame, guilt, fear, and anxiety around sex. They believe women think sex is bad. They believe that women think men who want sex are bad. If you have these kinds of SLBs you have probably worked very hard to hide any kind of sexual interest from the women you meet.

Here is the problem that has probably plagued you since you first noticed girls in middle school – you have been trying to hide your real reason for wanting to talk to them and date them: *you want to see them naked, but you don't want them to know.* Think about the success rate of that strategy for a moment; "If I hide my sexual agenda from a woman, maybe that will make her want to get naked with me."

Men who are comfortable having a strong sexual agenda exhibit minimal anxiety and maximum confidence when interacting with women. This is "mojo." Men who are uncomfortable with having a strong sexual agenda exhibit maximum anxiety and minimal confidence when interacting with women. This is NOT mojo.

Wanting to have sex doesn't make you a bad man. Your sexual interest is just the spark that gets the engine started. It is the knock on the door to a possibly great relationship (a great night of sex or something long-term). Most BDS get it backwards. They try to become a woman's friend first, while hiding any sexual interest. But, it is your initial sexual interest that actually starts you down the path to a potentially great relationship.

A BD fears that if he expresses sexual interest toward a woman, she will be disgusted and reject him. He is afraid that if he lets a woman know he wants to be more than friends, he will ruin the possibility of having a friendship. But, if expressing sexual interest ruins the friendship, there isn't much of a friendship.

By honoring your male sexual programming, you are increasing the odds of acting in such a way that will attract you to – and make you attractive to – some really great women. By repressing your sex drive, you are increasing the odds that you'll end up with some pretty messed up women.

Want a great relationship with a great woman? Engage her with your balls intact. Confidence is the number one aphrodisiac for women. It makes them feel safe. It turns them on. It makes them wet. Here's the good news: *You can confidently interact with women even when you don't feel confident.* Here are several things you can do to project confidence when you interact with women.

Confront Your SLBs

Odds are you have negative, distorted, and judgmental SLBs. You probably have a strong need to be perceived as nice. You have internalized messages from family and society that told you:

- Don't be a player.
- Be a gentleman.
- Don't hit on women.
- Don't be like all the other guys.
- Don't be like your father.
- Don't chase skirt.

You can use the information and tools from this book to confront and defeat these SLBs. You were born sexual; but religious, social, and familial messages have given you the idea that men are bad or sinful for being sexual. Additionally, you have probably internalized the SLB that women will be offended if you have sexual desire toward them.

Break the Catch 22

Most BDs believe they have to have confidence to get a woman, but they convince themselves that they need to experience success getting women in order to gain confidence. So without the confidence to experience success, how are they supposed to have the successes that would lead to confidence? This perceived *Catch 22* keeps them stuck, doing nothing, bemoaning both their lack of confidence and their lack of dating success.

Confidence is not necessarily a by-product of success. I've known successful people who never gained confidence and I've known people who lacked confidence yet became successful. Contrary to your inner-logic, success and confidence are not always related.

Confidence is the product of not caring too much about what people think. Lovingly not giving a fuck what people think allows you to interact with women and confidently engage them. Here are some ways to project confidence, even when you don't feel confident.

Talk to People Everywhere You Go

This is a practice for building confidence. The more you do it, the more confident you will feel. When one of the people you happen to be talking to is a woman you find attractive, you will just do what you have been doing every day. You will feel and appear confident. Don't wait until you see an attractive woman you want to talk to. Start talking to everyone now.

Set the Tone and Take the Lead

Most BDs are afraid of being controlling, *bad* men. Therefore, they approach women passively:

- I don't guess you'd want to go out with me sometime would you?
- What would YOU like to do?

This passively pleasing attitude doesn't make women think you are respectful. In fact, it makes them think you are wimpy. A healthy woman wants a man to take the lead. She doesn't want to be in control and she doesn't want a wimp. An integrated male can set the tone and take the lead without being controlling. Decide how you want to live your life and invite a woman to follow. Always remember: *A woman can't follow where a man doesn't lead.*

Tell, Don't Ask

Tell a woman to do what she already wants to do (even if she doesn't know it yet). This projects confidence and mojo. When you tell a woman what to do, with no attachment to outcome, you will appear to have greater status than her and this will turn her on.

Never ask a woman for her phone number. Say "give me your number." Never ask a woman if she wants to go out with you. Tell her "meet me Tuesday at 7:00 at Starbucks."

Never ask a woman if she wants to have sex. Tell her "take your clothes off and get in my bed." It is amazing how many women have told me "I can't believe you're telling me what to do" as they are unbuttoning their blouse!

You can do all of these things with assertiveness and playfulness without coming across as a controlling jerk.

Act

Action projects mojo. Sexual interest is communicated through action – not discussions. Don't talk about it, just do it!

A while back, in a group I led for single men, one of the guys mentioned that he had a date the next weekend with a woman he met speed dating. He had been talking about this woman in group for about four weeks. Even though they had only spent about an hour and half together (in addition to the seven-minute speed date), they had been talking on the phone for weeks, discussing the nature of their relationship, whether or not they would have sex, etc., etc.

I told the group member that it was time to "fuck more, talk less." This is always a good philosophy when it comes to taking the kind of action that projects confidence and mojo!

Don't Spend Too Much Time Listening to Women Talk About Their Problems

Many bad daters mistakenly believe that spending lots of time listening to women, asking them what they want, and letting them set the tone is effective foreplay. It isn't. This approach just lands you in the friend zone. While communication is important in building relationships, action is more powerful when it comes to building passion. *There is a reverse correlation between the amount of time a man spends listening to a woman talk about her problems and the amount of sex she will have with him.* I know this sounds counter-intuitive, but test it.

Tease Her

Healthy women love to be teased. It is a great way to raise a woman's interest level if she already has at least moderate interest in you. It really doesn't matter what you say or do, just tease her. Teasing and humor projects playful dominance and familiarity.

A while back, I took a survey and asked women why they are attracted to a man who can make them laugh. The common answer was that it projects confidence and intelligence. Many said it made them feel secure. One woman (who I was dating) responded matter-of-factly, "I don't care if a man is homely, if he makes me laugh, I'll do him!"

Touch Her

Touching a woman while you are talking to her demonstrates self-assurance and confidence. It is also a great way to test her interest level. Lean into her. Press your shoulder against hers. Gently but firmly grasp her arm just above her elbow and direct her through a crowded room. Touch the small of her back and gently pull her toward you. Take her hand when you cross a busy street. Lean in and kiss her on the cheek when you say goodbye.

Most BDs are afraid of offending a woman or being rejected by her. But, if a woman has high interest in you, she will like being touched by you.

Let Go of Attachment to Outcome

If you don't have any attachment to outcome, you can take all kinds of chances. You can risk looking foolish. You can crash and burn and live to tell about it. As soon as you get attached to outcomes, you'll become passive and risk-averse. Set the tone and take the lead. Touch her, tease her, tell her what to do. Don't spend too much time letting her ramble about her problems. Let go of attachment to outcome. Act more, think less.

Most of the principles I have presented in this chapter will be further explained and illustrated in Part 2 of the book. Keep reading.

PART 2: PERFECTING YOUR PRACTICE

The chapters in this half of *Dating Essentials for Men* focus on learning new skills and developing new daily routines. These skills and routines will help you meet and talk to women, and get what you want in dating, love and sex.

I promise that by the end of this section, you will be amazed by how easy it is to meet women, get their phone numbers, and get them into your bed. You will be amazed by how easy dating is when you apply some tried and true principles.

But, I should warn you: *Perfecting Your Practice* is where the rubber meets the road. In the *Mastering Your Mind* part of *Dating Essentials for Men*, you could easily read my tidbits of wisdom, nod your head, and say, "This is good stuff." *PYP* is where you actually have to get out there and *do something!*

When I first started putting the *Dating Essentials for Men* material together, I questioned myself, "There is already so much information on dating out there, and so many gurus teaching men to date, who am I to assume that my philosophy and approach will make a difference?" That was around 2007, and I figure the amount of dating resources and the number of dating gurus has tripled or quadrupled since then.

When I began creating *Dating Essentials for Men*, I came to the realization that it didn't really matter how much material was already out there, because the majority of bad daters are looking for a quick fix or magic bullet. Lonely, horny guys go online surfing for something that will change their love and sex lives without them having to anything different. The average BD will purchase boatloads of books and CDs, and sign up for classes, programs, and boot camps, looking for a quick, easy fix to their frustrations around women, love, and sex.

I also discovered that regardless of how much material the average BD buys and consumes, he will rarely push himself out of his comfort zone and apply what the material encourages him to do. He just keeps buying more material. This is what I mean when I say that *Perfecting Your Practice* is where everything gets *real*. If you really want something to be different in your life, you are going to have to do something different. Sometimes, doing something different is going to scare you to death. But, your anxieties won't actually kill you.

Everything I present in this section is doable. I know this, because not only have I – the original bad dater – done them all many times, I've watched countless other men practice these principles and have great dating success. *This shit works if you work it.*

Make a commitment to yourself. Vow to get out daily and practice the stuff I teach you in this book. Do the things that scare you the most – this is where the real growth and transformation occurs.

Perhaps it will be helpful to know, I didn't really write this book to help men meet women or get more love and sex. I wrote *Dating Essentials for Men* to help us grow as men, face our fears, get out of the nursery, embrace the challenging and fulfilling world of the masculine, and transform every aspect of our lives for the better.

But, when you practice what I teach, you will discover – as a pleasant side effect – that interacting with women, getting their numbers, getting laid, and finding a Really Great Woman, really isn't all that hard. *Dating Essentials for Men* has the power to transform your life in every way. The fact that you will also learn how to attract great women into your life is just the icing on the cake.

Let's do it!

CHAPTER 11: PAY ATTENTION TO DETAIL (SHE DOES)

God is in the details – Ludwig Mie's van der Rohe

Men find comfort in repetition and familiarity. We guys tend to get into ruts and do the same old thing over and over again. The average male can be happy wearing the same shirt and pair of pants day after day. A man can walk past piles of crap stacked around his house and hardly notice. He can get into a filthy car, toss another Burger King bag or Starbucks cup on the floor and leave it there for weeks.

These tendencies seem to be especially true for bad daters. Lack of focus, inattention to detail, procrastination, and problems following through are common traits of BDs. This pattern of neglect is apparent in many areas of their lives – in their homes, their cars, their behaviors, and their looks. This pattern is one of the reasons they have problems with dating and relationships.

If you want to be a successful dater and naturally attract women, you have to pay attention to the details in every area of your life.

Turning Women On

Do you know what turns women on? Many men assume it's having lots of money, being tall and good looking, having a full head of hair, being different from all the "jerks" out there, or listening to women talk about their problems for hours on end. These are all wrong answers.

Remember, as I shared in Chapter 9, women are sensual creatures. They experience life through their senses – touch, sight, taste, smell, and hearing. Their senses control their emotional state.

When a woman's senses are positively activated by a man, she experiences attraction. Even though women aren't as focused on a man's physical appearance as men are on a woman's, it still matters. Women are attracted to effort, confidence, potential, and attention to detail. These things all create a positive impact on their senses.

The purpose of this chapter is to get you to look at yourself and your environment through different eyes – the way a woman might look at things. The suggestions in this chapter will help you activate all of a woman's senses in a positive way. This information is meant to make you conscious of what you personally project to women and what your surroundings say about you. *Remember: Women notice the details, even if you don't.*

As I have previously asserted, many single men tend to look for some kind of formula or technique that will cause women to instantly fall for them. But, believe it not, seeking these magic bullets actually requires way too much work. Paying attention to detail not only improves the quality of your everyday life, it is also a powerful way to attract women to you naturally, without you having to depend on overworked pick-up routines, hypnosis, alcohol, or Nice Guy Seduction.

This chapter offers several easy ways to improve your life. It is somewhat of a shotgun approach, so don't get overwhelmed. Pick a few of the suggestions and start working on your life a little at a time. Before long, you will be amazed at how much easier it is to naturally attract women to you – just by the way you live! *If god is in the details, so is your Really Great Woman!*

Oh, and just a warning: Don't let your mind talk you into waiting until you have checked off every box in this chapter before you actually get out there and talk to women. Do both. Work on your life *while* you work on your dating skills.

Personal Grooming

You can't wait until you find a girlfriend to start paying attention to detail in your life. You never know when you might cross paths with a woman who could be a really great match. Every time you walk out your front door, look like you are going someplace important. Whether you are just running to the 7-11 or walking your dog in the park, look like you care.

Hair

You want a style that looks good, suits you, and is easy to maintain. If you are balding or have receding or thinning hair, go as short as possible. Either trim it close or shave your head. As hair thins or recedes, keeping it short minimizes the effect. Short, cropped hair looks confident and masculine. Never comb over any part – it is obvious (like when a woman pulls her long sweater over her ass hoping no one will notice how big it is). Comb-overs make you look insecure and geeky. Just go short.

If it has been a while since you changed or experimented with your hairstyle, go to a salon and get a really good style. The cut will cost more than you think it is worth, but a pro will know what looks best on you. Ask them to show you how to style it the way they did and ask what product they used. Then, when you get home, have a friend take pictures of your hair from several angles.

The next time you need a haircut, take the pictures to your local barber. They can make it look the same for less money if they have a picture for reference. Then, depending on how fast your hair grows, get it cut regularly (probably every three to five weeks). Style your hair and use your product. Keep it simple, but do it.

Teeth

Of course, you will floss and brush your teeth daily. Go to the dentist twice a year for cleaning. Talk with your dentist about the appearance of your teeth. Most guys would benefit from having their teeth whitened periodically, especially if they drink coffee or smoke (if you smoke or chew, quit).

If your teeth are crooked or uneven, consider orthodontics or veneers. Veneers can be a great way to improve the look of your teeth at a reasonable price. Your smile says volumes about you, so make it electric. If bad or yellowing teeth make you too uptight to smile, take care of it. You are worth it.

Just a few years ago, I invested in veneers and crowns for my teeth. I had never really liked my smile. Since that time, I smile freely and people tell me I look happier and younger – and much more attractive. I suggest you save yourself a ton of money and plan a dental vacation to Mexico.

Your Body

Go to the gym regularly and get yourself into shape. Slim down or build up. You will undoubtedly feel more confident if you are lean and strong. There is no reason not to be. Being and staying fit will help you live longer and improve your mood. Most women aren't looking for a bodybuilder. They just want a man who takes care of himself, looks good in his clothes, and is comfortable getting naked. So, if you have been telling yourself that no woman would want you because you are too fat or too skinny, do something about it. No more excuses!

In addition to being *sensual creatures*, I also asserted in Chapter 9 that women are *security seeking creatures*. These two things – living through their senses and wanting to feel safe – are the core of female attraction and arousal. In order for a woman to feel safe with a man, she has to know that he is in control of himself. This is the reason for their *shit tests*. They have to test and see if you have your shit together before they will feel safe with you.

One of the first signals you send about whether or not you are in control of yourself is what you project with your body. This is why you need to take good care of yourself, eat healthy, and workout regularly. If you are overweight or sunken-chested, women will immediately see you as a man who doesn't have control of himself. This is a complete turn-off for the kind of women you want to attract. Okay, let's continue with the details.

Fingernails

Many women have told me that this is one of the first things they notice about a man. If your nails are dirty, ragged, or too long, it's a turn off for many women. Keep your nails trimmed and cleaned. Treat yourself to a manicure every few months.

Facial Hair

If you have facial hair, keep it groomed and trimmed. I know that Tom Cruise and Brad Pitt can get away with looking like street bums, but most of us can't. You can buy clippers with depth guides to help you keep your facial hair neat and proportional. You can also ask a good stylist what looks good on your face. What we guys think looks good is not always accurate. A little facial stubble can look stylish, but don't use it as an excuse to avoid shaving regularly.

Manscaping

Body hair is masculine. You don't have to go through the waxing agony of Steve Carell's character in *The 40-Year-Old Virgin,* but you should keep your body hair under control. Trimmers with a guide can come in handy for keeping chest and back hair nicely trimmed. There is no need to look like a shaggy bear after six months of hibernation.

As we guys get older, we lose hair on our heads and grow it everywhere else. At least once a week, trim the hairs in your nose and ears. You might even need to get your eyebrows trimmed. Women really notice this (they tell me all the time to be sure and tell men to pay attention to these details). You can use a small battery powered trimmer made for this or small scissors with blunt ends. I regularly get my ears waxed and my eyebrows trimmed by a professional. It doesn't cost much, doesn't take long, and makes a big difference.

Cologne

I personally believe that the natural smell of male pheromone is the best scent on a man. If you like to wear cologne, take a woman shopping with you and have her help you pick a good scent for your body. Then use a light touch. Too much fragrance is a turn off. Don't slap it on or bathe in it. Spray a gentle mist from arms' length on your bare chest only, not your clothes.

My rule of thumb is: *The only person who should be able to smell your cologne is a woman who has her nose pressed against your chest.* Since smell is the strongest memory center in the brain, your scent will trigger good feelings in your woman every time you are close to her.

Overall Appearance

Be willing to spend money on your appearance. Dental work, contacts, Lasik eye surgery (one of the best gifts I ever gave myself), minor plastic surgery, even just getting a facial or manicure is a great way to improve your looks and make you feel good about yourself. This doesn't make you vain. You don't have to go overboard, but invest in yourself. Every guy I have ever known who has done something to improve his overall look has felt great about the investment he made in himself. Most guys wish they had done it sooner.

Fashion

They come runnin' just as fast as they can, Coz every girl crazy 'bout a sharp dressed man. – ZZ Top

Develop your own style. This means giving some thought to what looks good on you and what makes you feel good. Fashion is a conscious process. Find a basic look that works well for you, whether it is jeans and a t-shirt, chinos and polo shirts, or nice trousers and button-down shirts.

You don't need a lot of clothes. But, when it comes to the basics, buy quality. Your own personal fashion touch can include adding just a few nice things to your basic look. Like an expensive pair of shoes, a classic blazer, a great pair of aviators, or a nice watch (I get compliments on my Omega all the time). Just one or two nice things added to your wardrobe makes everything else look better. Women notice the little details, as well as the quality (you do want a woman who recognizes quality, don't you?).

I frequently poll women on what they tend to notice first about a man's fashion. The most common answers are: watch, shoes and overall sense of style. Mostly, does he look comfortable in his skin and clothes?

Your personal style tells a story about you and your life. When I travel, I often buy fashion accessories. I've bought shoes in New York City, a silver ring in Mexico, and a Burberry hat from Harrod's in London. All have a story. When a woman comments on one of these accessories, I can tell her the story. Not only does it add a little flair to my basic wardrobe, it gives me a chance to tell women about my life.

As I mentioned, women tell me that one of the first things they notice about a man (along with his hands and fingernails) is his shoes. Invest in good shoes. I remember the first time I paid over $200 for a pair of shoes. This was hard to do, but those shoes lasted seven or eight years. They really only cost me about $25 per year. I resoled them twice. If you wear leather shoes, find a shoeshine stand and get your shoes polished regularly. You'll find it's a nice treat, extends the life of your shoes, and keeps you looking sharp.

Even if you tend to just wear Vans or Olukai flip flops (both of which I basically live in here in Mexico), scuffed up or overly worn shoes send a terrible message to women. Keep your shoes clean, looking good, and in good repair. Get rid of them before they look worn out.

Asking for Help

Most men need help for what looks good on them. Ask someone to go shopping with you who has good taste. This can be a man or a woman. If you know a guy who dresses sharp, ask him to help. Ask a woman who has good taste, but I don't recommend your mom or sister. Ask your *personal consultant* to help you find things that can update your wardrobe, that look good on you, and will make a positive impression on women. Again, a few basics and a few nice things are all you need.

Have this person go through your closet with you and help you get rid of things that don't fit, are out of style, or are worn out. One of the biggest mistakes men tend to make is wearing clothes that are too big for them. Unless you are a professional rapper, baggy and oversize clothing sends a negative message to women. Let your consultant help you make a list of things that you can add to your wardrobe over time. This will let you stay on a budget and find things on sale. Go through your closet twice per year and repeat the process – get rid of things that don't fit, are out of style, or you haven't worn in a year.

Clothes make the man. Naked people have little or no influence on society. – Mark Twain

Your Home

Women see your home as a reflection of you. The more your personal space is well-organized, clean, and sensually pleasing, the more attractive a woman will find you. Women can't help this response, it's just the way they are programmed.

In my single days, when I would bring a woman to my apartment for the first time, I could see her sensual response. She wandered from room to room (including my bedroom), oohing and ahhing about the colors, my art, my candles, my furnishings, my bed. I'd watch her relax and touch things. She usually asked two questions, "Did you do this yourself?" and "Is it always this clean?" (When is the last time a woman asked you either of those questions about your home?)

If your house is messy, dirty, disorganized or generally uninviting, you won't want to bring women there. Women won't want to come to a messy, dirty house. If your home looks like a college dorm room or it's scattered with a few mismatched pieces of furniture that your ex-wife left you in the divorce, this will be a turn off for women. Remember, women notice the details and they want to know you've put some thought and effort into how you live.

There are other benefits as well. By creating a warm and inviting home (and keeping it clean and clutter free), you will feel good about your personal space and enjoy being there. No matter where I've lived, I have created a beautiful, comfortable space that makes me feel relaxed and happy. I've always enjoyed opening my door when I come home and experiencing the feeling of contentment that my space gives me.

The second benefit is that you won't hesitate to bring women home and they will enjoy being there. Odds are they will want to keep coming back. When I was in my dating heyday, it was not unusual for the women to come to my place 80% – 90% of the time rather than me going to their place. I never even saw the homes of a number of women I dated. They all liked hanging out at my place.

Asking for Help, Part II

If you are feeling overwhelmed about where to start or how to make this happen, don't worry. Ask for help. Ask someone you know who has good decorating taste. Either that, or hire a professional. I think I have good taste, but having a professional decorator has made all the difference in my home. Many men need to start this process with a professional organizer. If necessary, hire someone who can help you get all of your stuff organized and stored.

I suggest that you hire a house cleaner at least once a month. Then maintain that look yourself. Keep sinks, tubs and toilets clean. Vacuum and dust at least every other week. Clean windows and mirrors every month or so. Keep your bathroom clean. No towels on the floor. No butt hairs or pee spots on the toilet. Keep your refrigerator clean. Make your bed every day. Keep your dishes done and countertops clean. Pick your clothes up. Every time you leave your house, leave it clean and tidy. You never know when you might want to bring someone home with you.

All of the information above applies if you live in a large house, a tiny apartment, or a room in your parent's home. Don't use anything as an excuse to avoid creating a warm, comfortable living space.

Your Car

Your car also makes an impression and says a lot about you to a woman. Men can get caught up into thinking they have to have a nice car to impress a woman. This isn't true, so don't use it as an excuse to not date. As a single man, I drove a Jetta, a Subaru station wagon, a BMW, a Ford Explorer, and a Mercedes. I found that the kind of car I drove had absolutely nothing to do with how successfully I dated.

No matter what you drive, keep it clean. Wash the exterior as often as it needs. Always keep the interior clean. No garbage on the floors, no crap on the dashboard, no piles of stuff in the back seat. If you need to carry things in your car, keep some duffle bags or storage boxes in your trunk and put your stuff there. Don't smoke in your car. If you have a cracked windshield or are missing a hubcap, fix it. Those are the kind of things that are easy to put off and live with. They are also the details that women notice first when they get in your car.

Personal Behaviors

If your own personal behavior is irritating, distracting, or crass, then it doesn't matter how much style you have or how great your car and home look. I've noticed that many BDs have behaviors or mannerisms that quickly turn a woman off. Since these mannerisms are often unconscious, ask a couple of close friends to tell you if you do anything that might irritate or distract.

These socially inappropriate or distracting behaviors might include: belching or farting in public, picking or wiping your nose, talking too much, being overly opinionated or a know-it-all, interrupting, avoiding eye contact, scratching your balls, and drinking too much. Since most people won't just tell you that you do these things, you'll have to ask. And since most of these habits are unconscious, you will have to consciously work to overcome them. Have your friends give you a predetermined signal if you are doing them in public.

Be Yourself

The most important aspect of style is being yourself. None of the suggestions in this chapter mean anything if you aren't being yourself. Don't try and be something you aren't. Don't try and impress. Have fun, be yourself, enjoy the adventure. Remember, if paying attention to detail is where you'll find god, it is where you'll find your goddess as well.

CHAPTER 12: USE THE INTERNET TO YOUR ADVANTAGE

Dating is a numbers game.

Technology and the internet have opened countless doors for men and women to meet. Not so long ago, taking out a personal ad was considered something only losers did. Now, internet dating has become commonplace, with very little stigma attached. In fact, the internet has pretty much become the new meeting place for singles seeking partners. There are numerous ways to tap into the internet as a dating tool.

- Websites like Match.com, Cupid.com, Plentyoffish.com, and Yahoo.com allow you to post a profile and browse the profiles of prospective dates.
- E-harmony.com provides a similar service with more structure and the goal of helping you find your "soul-mate."
- Sites like Adultfriendfinder.com will help you locate women who are primarily seeking sexual encounters.
- Facebook.com serves as a way to connect with peers on many different levels, not just romantically.
- Meetup.com provides information about different kinds of social groups listed by city.
- Chat rooms and interest groups allow men and women from around the world to meet and chat around specific topics, games, etc.
- Craigslist.com can be used for just about anything.

- Tinder, Hinge, and Bumble allow you to find women right around the corner.

Online dating and hookup change so quickly that by the time you read the list of resources above, they may be outdated.

A Tool, Not a Crutch

When it comes to internet dating, the men with whom I work tend to fall into three categories. Some have never done it and find it a little intimidating or stigmatized. Others have tried it in the past but claim, "It didn't work" (a common refrain of BDs who try many things just once before giving up). Then, there are those who use the internet as their only avenue for meeting women because it is less frightening than actually talking to them in public.

The internet is a great tool for meeting women – a tool that opens many doors that might not ever open in the course of a man's daily life. Meeting women online is a great way to get started with dating. Dating websites and apps provide a simple and straightforward way for a man to insert himself into the dating world. Writing a personal profile tends to force a man to evaluate his life in a way that allows him to see his strengths and weaknesses.

There are drawbacks to internet dating, though. It can become a crutch to avoid actually dealing with women in the flesh. A man can easily get caught up in endless messaging with women whom he has never met, spending every spare moment swiping left or right, or getting involved in long distance relationships that have no hope of ever working out. Online dating allows a man to stay at home in front of a computer or on a mobile app while deluding himself that he is actually having a life.

Finally, *internet dating is inorganic.* Online, people get focused on things like age, body type, and income; and use a fuzzy two-inch picture to make choices about whom they will or will not contact. Typically, when people meet each other in public situations, these factors aren't as significant.

As I have stated many times in this book, I am a big advocate of getting out of the house, expanding your route, and talking to people everywhere you go. This is the real world. This is where you meet people in the flesh. This is where doors open. This is where miracles happen.

The internet is a great tool to meet people and expand your world, but it is just that, a tool, not a crutch. Online dating is one more way to get out of the house and meet women. My suggestion is that if you are going to use online dating, it should only make up about 25% of your total dating effort. The rest can be from things like speed dating, singles mixers, church groups, classes, social groups, and from getting out of the house and talking to people everywhere you go (as we will explore further in upcoming chapters).

Low Frustration Level

Before we get into some ways to effectively use internet dating, let me briefly address the issue of "I tried it before and it didn't work for me." As I said, this is a common lament of bad daters. One fairly consistent trait of BDs (and maybe one of the primary reasons they *are* BDs) is a *low tolerance for frustration.* These men tend to give up easily. They abandon a principle or tool the first time it doesn't work or the first time they get rejected. If at first they don't succeed, bad daters often quit and never try again.

Approaching women, talking to them, asking for phone numbers, risking rejection, going on dates, initiating sex, and breaking up – all create anxiety. There is no way around it. *BDs hate anxiety* and they will do almost anything to avoid it. So, if they try something once and it doesn't go well the first time, they just claim: "It didn't work for me" or "I tried it once and crashed and burned." Then they can justify avoiding doing anything that might make them feel anxious.

If this describes you, I encourage you to *lean into your anxiety.* Try some new things. Take some chances. Take some risks. Keep doing things until you get better at them. Keep doing them until the anxiety dissipates. If you do something and don't get positive results the first time, try again. Try doing it a little different. Try doing it in a different context. Try doing it without attachment to outcome.

Dating is a numbers game and you are going to fail a lot more than you succeed. Successful daters know this. They persevere in the face of failure and rejection. You are going to hear me say things like "lean into the fear" and "get to rejection quickly." These are the keys to success.

Effort = Success (effort is success)!

If you've tried online dating, speed dating, dance lessons, or whatever else in the past and "It just didn't work," then try again. And again. Experiment. Try different things and different approaches. This is one of the great things about internet dating, you can keep trying new things, while literally reinventing yourself over and over again.

Creating a Life

When I first tried online dating, creating my personal profile was a revealing process. Since adolescence, I believed that being a *great guy* was sufficient enough to get a woman to notice me and want to go out with me. When I went online and began reading the profiles, I had a "holy shit" experience. I realized that just showing up and being *nice* wasn't going to cut it in the online dating world. But more than that, the process of writing my online profile illuminated the reality that, for some years, I had built my life around other people. Take away those people, and there wasn't a lot of *me* left to sell.

Therefore, *creating a profile was an exercise in evaluating my life.* The process forced me to decide what I wanted my life to look like, what I needed to change, what I needed to add and what fears I needed to face. Creating a profile also required me to think about what kind of woman I wanted to attract and what it was going to take to attract her.

As we talk about how to create an effective dating profile, in many ways we will be exploring how to help you create the kind of life you want, and how to attract the kind of women you want in your life. So, the first thing I am going to suggest you do as you build an online profile is that you make a list of all of your interests, passions, activities and hobbies. If the list seems a little one dimensional or limited, make a second list of all the things you think you might like to do.

I made such a list when I developed my first online profile. I came across this same list about three years later and discovered that I had done about half a dozen of the things on my list. Three or four of them have become regular parts of my life. I also realized that I had tried a few things that weren't on my list. After finding my list, I began to make plans to try a few more things I hadn't gotten around doing. The result: My life is now fuller and more interesting than it was before I created my first online profile.

Create a Dating Profile

In this chapter we will primarily discuss creating a profile for dating sites like Match, OkCupid, PlentyOfFish, and eHarmony. We will discuss username, headline, pictures, and the other parts of your profile. We'll also discuss contacting women on these sites and how to initiate meeting for a coffee date. This is by no means an exhaustive approach to all the ways you can use the internet to meet women, but it is a good start.

If you haven't already done so, sign up for an online dating site. Pick one that is either free or that allows you to sign up for a trial period. Begin by exploring the site to see how it works. Look over other men's profiles on the site. Pay attention to what gets your attention and what doesn't. As you look at men's profiles, keep in mind that *women don't use a man's profile so much to choose him, they use it to rule him out.*

A profile shouldn't scream, "pick me, pick me." The goal of the profile isn't to impress a woman or make you look like the best man available. A woman isn't going to read your profile and decide you are the man of her dreams. It is just an introduction. Typically, a woman will look at the big picture and see if something about the man strikes her fancy. She doesn't need to know about every accomplishment or every interest you have. Your profile doesn't have to jump out at a woman, it just has to give her a little snapshot of who you are, and do something to create a little buzz. You don't have to stand out from the crowd (more is not better), you just have to get your foot in the door.

Username

Most online dating sites have you choose a username. Be creative. A woman isn't going to pick you based on your username, but she probably won't be inspired by usernames like, *"bob1154"*, or *"Seattle07."* Pick something that shows some personality, yet can't be misinterpreted as negative or sleazy.

Try combinations that incorporate your first name, your job, one of your better attributes or a hobby. Pick a whimsical or clever name. Just be careful about using humor or terms so obscure that the average person won't get them. I would discourage you from using engineering, computer, Star Wars, or Lord of the Rings references (whereas poking a little fun at yourself is okay, i.e., *"SciFiGeek"*). Have fun, but don't overthink it. You can change your username as often as you want.

Headline

Your headline is a great way to attract attention to your profile. Since your headline is one of the first things other members notice, it's a way to make a good first impression. Like a username, a headline probably won't be the determining factor as to whether or not a woman will contact you. But, you also don't want it to turn her off. On most online sites, when you email a woman, your username and headline will be the only part of the email she initially sees.

Your headline is a great place to present something unique about you, highlight one of your interests or be a little clever or funny. I personally like to use headlines that paint a picture that creates a positive feeling with the reader. Some examples: *"Toes in the sand," "Knee deep in Vail powder,"* or *"Sailing the crystal blue waters of the Caribbean."*

When I created my first profile, I looked at some profiles on Match.com for guys my age in my area. Most were dull, boring and predictable. Only a few were interesting and clever.

Dull and boring:

- *Hi*
- *Let's talk*
- *GRAPHIX GUY*
- *Giving and receiving love*
- *Angels do appear on Valentine's day* (gag me)
- *Seeking someone special*
- *As you wish*
- *Easygoing*
- *Looking for you*

- *Greetings*

If you were a woman, would you get excited about any of these? Clever or intriguing:

- *Not your typical "techie"(first picture* was him in a wetsuit doing something active.)
- *Style is knowing who you are, what you want to say and not giving a damn.*
- *Rare & Precious Gem Sought to Team for Brilliance, or to just help me write better poetry & headlines?* (I clicked on this one to use as an example of a bad headline, then saw the whole thing – kind of clever. First picture was him on the slopes in ski goggles.)

Photos

The rules regarding pictures are pretty basic. First, you should have some. No woman will click on your profile without them. Use more than one and less than four. The pictures should all be high quality. Photos that are fuzzy, out of focus, poorly lit or too far away are all distracting and do nothing to make you look good. Have a professional or a friend take pictures of you in various situations. Try to avoid looking overly posed.

Don't use pictures where you have cropped out an ex-girlfriend – no hanging arms. I'm not sure why, but women do the *dangling arm* thing all time. I can't count how many photos I've seen with a woman and part of an arm or hand showing on her side (and the rest of the body is missing). The other thing women seem to do quite a bit is post a shot of them with a girlfriend or two having fun. It often leaves you wondering which one is her, while hoping it is the better looking one of the group.

Your *primary* photo is the first thing a woman will see on your profile. Your picture should be a recent, quality head shot of you. Dating sites will crop a photo of you to use as your primary, but you will get better results if you upload a head shot (though not one of you in a suit and tie you might have for business use).

Upload one or two more shots that show your full body. One of these can be of you doing something active. No pictures of sunsets, mountains, etc. A picture of you with your pet, your kayak, snow board, or your Harley are okay because they show things that are important to you. (Several women have told me they are not particularly drawn to photos of men with fish or men drinking beer with their buddies.) Oh yeah, leave your shirt on and no *dick* shots (women can get away with showing body parts but men can't).

In general, women are not as influenced by a man's physical appearance as we guys are of a woman's. *Physical appearance is important to women, but remember, for most attraction is based primarily on how a man makes them feel.* Your profile pictures are important, but you don't have to look like Liam Hemsworth, Vin Diesel, or Usher to get a woman's attention. If you are going to be online for a little while, change your primary picture every couple of weeks. A woman may notice you the second time she sees your profile if you have a different photo.

Your Personal Profile

Don't put pressure on yourself to create the perfect essay. Start by simply letting the reader know about you. Think of what you'd say in an email to a long-lost friend you haven't talked to in ten years. How would you bring them up to speed on your life? Describe your typical day, what your personality is like, and what you like to do for fun.

Look at your life. What do you want to present of yourself? This is where the list I mentioned earlier comes in handy. Use it as a guide to describe yourself and what you like to do. You can even mention things you would like to try or learn how to do.

Seemingly insignificant details in your profile, no matter how small, can stick in a woman's mind and create interest. Mention, for example, that you do the *New York Times* crossword puzzle every Sunday, that last summer you took a trip to Ireland, that you are training for your first triathlon, that you enjoy a certain neighborhood bistro or that you are learning Italian. *When describing these things about you, be specific. Create a visual and sensual picture in the reader's mind.*

- Instead of: "I like to dance," write "You'll find me dancing salsa every Saturday night at the Century Ballroom."

- Instead of "I like to eat out," write, "I can't resist the nachos at 520 on Main Street."
- Instead of "I love to travel," write, "My favorite escape is sitting under a palapa, sipping margaritas on the beach in Puerto Vallarta."

Paint word pictures. Remember that women are sensual creatures. If you appeal to their senses, you will appeal to their hearts (and other regions).

In general, don't explain what you do for a living unless your job is really unique. If your career is an important part of your life, it is okay to indicate this. If you are passionate about what you do, tell the reader why. Just don't go into deep, technical details. Never say how much you make, even if the profile template on the dating site specifically asks.

Write enough in your profile to show you put some effort into it, but not so much that the woman loses interest and moves on. When writing your profile, the first paragraph is crucial. It might be the only thing a woman reads before she clicks the back button. Keep it short. Make it punchy and intriguing. Break up the remaining paragraphs by keeping them short.

Don't try to impress. Be yourself. That's what you want women to be attracted to anyway. Use a little humor. Have a little edge. Avoid the temptation to present yourself as a Nice Guy. I've read some men's profiles that actually looked like an advertisement for the Nice Guy Syndrome. Remember, women aren't attracted to *nice*.

Who You'd Like to Meet

Your profile should also describe what you are looking for in a woman. Avoid being so specific that very few women would qualify. This can also make you look picky and shallow. If you are attracted to confidence in women or women who like the outdoors, say so. Negative language ("I don't want … , I don't like … .") makes your profile a magnet for exactly the types you're trying to avoid. This also makes you seem whiney and negative.

Your profile is the place to specify what you do want in a relationship, not what you don't want. Turn any of your negative statements into positives. Instead of saying "I'm tired of head games," which translates to, "I've got a chip on my shoulder," try, "Honesty is the most important thing in a relationship for me."

I have found that many BDS seek a woman who can boost their low sense of self-worth. While it is normal for men to be attracted to healthy, attractive women, seeking a woman who is much younger than you and much more attractive than you makes you look insecure. Women reading your profile will probably be turned off if you're 40, yet you only want to date women 20 to 32, or if you're clearly overweight but specify slender women only. When a guy's desired match makes him seem judgmental – like he doesn't even want to date someone his own age – it comes across in a negative way. How would it come across to you if a woman said she only dated rich guys who can take her to nice places?

After you complete your profile, have at least three people look it over (at least one woman). Make sure there are no spelling, grammatical, or punctuation errors. Every month or so, change your profile around. Play with it. Experiment. Check out other online profiles to get ideas. Change your primary picture. Change your username and headline. Keep your profile fresh and interesting. Most importantly, have fun.

The Invitation

Consider it your job to set the tone and test for interest. A reality of online dating is that women don't have to work that hard at it. They don't have to be proactive. After posting a couple of sentences (just a single paragraph if they are attractive), they can sit back and let the contacts pour in. All they have to do is weed out the guys who don't interest them or who obviously didn't read their profiles.

Some women will "wink" at you, but don't count on women making the first contact (unless they are new to online dating). If a young, attractive woman contacts you and says she is looking for a nice guy like you, it is probably a come-on from a porn site.

Once you have completed your profile, it is time to start browsing the women's profiles. Some online sites will send you prospective matches. All have some kind of search engine. Go looking, keeping in mind the qualities you are looking for in a prospective mate. When you find a woman who intrigues you, write her a short email. Never *wink*, it is passive and forces the woman to set the tone. When contacting prospective matches, keep it simple. Being a little clever and personal can only help. Most importantly, show that you have read her profile – not just looked at her photos.

The goal of your initial email is to direct her to your profile. Therefore, all you have to do is get her attention, you're not trying to sell her. Just invite her to take a look at you. If the woman responds to your email, I suggest responding fairly soon with an invitation to meet for coffee, a drink, or a walk in the park. I suggest initially meeting for a simple face-to-face date for a number of reasons.

First and foremost, the purpose of dating is to get to know a person's nature. Telling her to meet for something casual is a way of setting the tone and taking the lead. A simple face-to-face date is the ideal next step for getting to know her a little better. It is also an effective way to test for interest. This is also a way to see how flexible and available she is. The initial date is an ideal way to get to rejection as quickly as possible.

Meet as soon as possible. Keep chatting to a minimum. Proposing to meet right away is a way of avoiding one of the biggest pitfalls of online dating – too much chatting via email and phone before meeting. There are at least four major pitfalls of texting and chatting too much before meeting:

- You really can't get to know much about a person's nature on the phone or over email. You can only discover a person's true nature by observing them in person. In the past, I have chatted a little by email before meeting. I would be intrigued by a woman's sense of humor and playfulness, only to meet her in person and wonder if her roommate wrote her emails.
- It is easy to fall in love with a person you have never met. This is a recipe for disaster (try breaking up with a woman you have gotten close to via the phone and email only to discover on your first date that she is a complete turn off!).
- Chatting is an effective way to play it safe (BDs like this).

- Some women who respond to your email may suggest chatting for a little while before meeting. This is the woman setting the tone from the beginning – never a good idea. Often these women are just looking for male attention and not really wanting to connect.

When a woman responds with interest to your initial email, immediately begin to work out the plans for meeting. Suggest a day, time, and place to meet for coffee or a drink. If she proposes an alternative day, tell her you will have to get back to her. Wait at least a day and contact her again. If her proposed day and time works for you, set up the date. If you want to test how much she needs to be in control, suggest a completely different time. When the day, time and location have been established, no more emailing or phone chatting before the date.

Swiping Right

One of my No More Mr. Nice Guy certified coaches is a master at using Tinder and Bumble. He believes he has found the key to success on these mobile dating apps. He has a very basic hack to use when swiping right on a woman's profile or when replying to a woman who has swiped right on yours. Here is his simple, but well-tested response:

"Amber (use <u>her</u> name), you animal, what are you doing here?"

He says a woman used this on him one time and he has used it ever since. He swears by its effectiveness in getting things heated up quickly.

Time to Get Busy

Okay, you've made a connection and set up a time and place to meet. It's time to move dating offline and out into the real world. Keep reading for what comes next.

CHAPTER 13: COMMIT TO GOING OUT WITH 12 WOMEN IN 12 WEEKS

Practice makes perfect.

You have probably heard this truism since childhood. If you want to do anything well and if you want to do it confidently, you have to practice – a lot. Like every other skill, this theorem applies to dating. As I've mentioned, many BDS have a low frustration level and give up easily when initial attempts at dating don't go well. As a result, they never get good at the skill sets required for successful dating, nor do they develop confidence.

I don't know about you, but anything that I ever got halfway good at (baseball, soccer, multiplication tables, guitar, writing code, salsa, therapy, public speaking) required two things: a teacher, and lots of practice of the fundamental skills. In time, these skills became second nature.

When it comes to dating, most of us never had a good teacher. Therefore, whatever skills we developed probably weren't very effective. Because we didn't have a good skill set to work from, we didn't have much success. And, since positive experiences tend to motivate us to keep practicing, most of us gave up quickly when we didn't have immediate success. The *Perfecting Your Practice* section of *Dating Essentials for Men* is geared toward teaching you the skills you need to get the love and sex you want. This chapter in particular outlines a strategy that will push you to practice what you are learning.

I am going to propose a challenge to you to help you most effectively apply and practice the principles and skills I am teaching you in this book. Whether you are meeting women online, with a dating app, or by any of the other strategies I share with you, I am proposing a deep dive. The strategy of this chapter is simple: *Challenge yourself to go on 12 dates with 12 different women over the next 12 weeks.*

The 12/12 challenge is great for men who have never dated much, lack confidence, need to practice dating skills, and/or have been avoiding dating and need a jump start. The beauty of the 12/12 challenge is that it is simple. There is no agenda or desired outcomes. The 12/12 allows you to go on all kinds of dates with all kinds of women. And, while doing so, you get to practice everything you are learning in this book.

The 12/12 works to get you going and keep you going, partly because it requires a public commitment on your part. You make a commitment to yourself and a commitment to friends and family who are going to help you find some of the women you are going to ask out over the next 12 weeks.

For the 12/12 to work, you can't half-ass it. You can't put it off and wait until the last minute and try to cram 12 dates into five days. You have to commit. Even if your mind is trying to talk you out of making such a commitment, do it anyway. Commit now. It doesn't get easier if you wait and make the commitment next week or the week after. Commit even if you are busy, scared, and have no idea where you will find 12 women to date (no one knows where they are going to find 12 women to date when they begin the 12/12 challenge).

How The 12/12 Works

Since this is for practice, it doesn't matter what kind of women you date. You can ask out your second cousin, women with nose rings, fat women, grandmothers, lesbians – it doesn't matter. It is just practice; any woman will do (Avoid stupid women and feminazis – you'll spend an hour in hell!).

This strategy frees you up to focus your energy on practicing your skills rather than investing your attention and energy in trying to get your date to like you. This will also help you get your ego out of the way. Many BDs insist they only want to date very attractive women. If this is you, this is a great way to ensure that you never date at all, and consequently, never develop skills or confidence.

Dating is scary. Your mind will come up with all kinds of creative ways to avoid feeling the anxiety that comes with asking women out on dates. The 12/12 helps bypass this because you can ask out *low anxiety* women. As you start feeling more confident, you can mix in more dates with women who raise your anxiety level a little bit. The 12/12 pushes your ego out of the way because you'll be dating women you would never ordinarily consider asking out. You might actually find that these women are interesting and good company (maybe better company than the hotties your ego would like to see hanging on your arm).

Letting Go of Attachment to Outcome

Let me ask you a question. Why do you look at women? Check them out? Talk to them? Ask them out? You do all these things because you have an intention: *you want to see them naked.* In other words, you want to find a girlfriend and/or you want to have sex. That is your agenda. A less *animal* or *base* rationalization for talking to women is just the BS your mind tells you to avoid thinking you're one of those creepy guys who hit on women and only want to use them for sex.

Your desire to see a woman's breasts, touch her body, and put your penis in her vagina is what motivates you to face your fears and approach them. Unfortunately, this agenda tends to escalate your anxiety as well. This diminishes the likelihood of you acting in a way that might help you achieve your goals. *By removing the typical agenda, the 12/12 helps reduce much of the typical anxiety around dating.* If your anxiety is reduced, you are more likely to go on more dates, be yourself, and practice the skills you are learning in this book.

The 12/12 allows you to practice:

- Approaching women
- Asking women out
- Having conversations with women
- Testing
- Setting the tone/taking the lead

- The 3Ts (touch, tease, and tell)
- Being clear and direct
- Being a good ender

Several men who have taken the 12/12 challenge have found a woman they wanted to keep dating during the challenge. That's okay. The rule (or strong suggestion) is you still have to finish the 12/12. The woman you want to keep seeing only counts as one date.

The remainder of this chapter will focus on how to implement the 12/12. We will discuss the basics of how to ask a woman out, what to do on a first date, how to be a good ender, and how to find the 12 women. This information can be applied to any dating context, whether you are doing the 12/12 or just dating in general.

Have a Plan

Let's assume that you have made some initial contact with the woman you want to ask out. You've met her online, at a coffee shop, or a class. Maybe a friend or family member made the introduction. Depending on the context, you can invite her out by phone or email. Doing it face-to-face or over the phone is ideal, but it is okay to leave an email or voicemail message with your invitation. Here are the essentials:

You must have a plan – know when and where you want to meet her. This is the starting point. The plan can be adjusted as you talk, but having a plan is a powerful way to start by setting the tone and taking the lead. Never propose that the two of you "go out sometime." Never ask something like, "are you free this weekend?" Do not ask a woman out until you have a specific plan.

The initial date should always be on a weekday (any time) or Sunday afternoon. Never, ever plan a first date on one of the prime date nights (Friday & Saturday). You don't want to leave the impression that you have nothing to do on these nights besides have coffee with a woman you don't know.

Tell – never ask! Ironically, "asking" a woman out puts you in a one down position to the woman. Telling her when and where to meet you raises your status in her eyes and will make you look more attractive, confident and desirable. I suggest a couple ways of doing this. One is to say something like, "Let's meet for coffee Thursday night at the Starbucks on Main Street. Meet me there at 7.00 PM." A second approach is to say something like, "I'm going to be down at Carlo's Tuesday night listening to this great Latin band. You should join me." This makes you look like an interesting guy who has an interesting life. You are inviting her to join you in your interesting life.

If you can't share your plan face to face or directly over the phone and have to leave a message, I suggest saying something like, "Sarah, this is Jim. We chatted last Sunday at Bill's party. Let's meet for coffee on Thursday and continue our conversation. Give me a call (or message me) and I'll give you the details." Whether or not she calls you back is a demonstration of her interest. If she calls, she has high interest – tell her your plan. If she doesn't call back, she has low interest – move on.

Remember, every interaction you have with a prospective date is a test of her nature. How well she follows, how flexible she is, how spontaneous she is. She will be testing you too. If she is a healthy woman, she doesn't want a guy she can push around. She doesn't want a guy who will do anything to please her and accommodate her. She will have to test to find out what kind of guy you are.

I introduced the concept of *shit tests* in Chapter 11. I have heard plenty of men complain about these tests. That's because we men typically misunderstand their purpose. Women don't test to be *shitty*. They test to see if we have our *shit* together. As security seeking creatures, women want to know if they can both trust and depend on you. As one of my ex-wives used to state every time I failed one of her shit tests, *"If* I don't know you can stand up *to* me, how will I ever know that you will stand up *for* me?" She was right!

A healthy woman doesn't want to be the strongest person in the room. She wants to be able to trust you. She has to test to find out if she can. If you let the woman climb into the driver's seat from the very beginning, you will probably never get her out. You have failed the test. This is the beginning of the end. She now has two options: lose interest in you or take control. You leave her no other choice when you get passive and let her set the tone.

Okay, once the day, time, and location have been established, get off the phone and stop texting. No more contact or chatting before the date.

The Date

Your first contact with a woman usually serves one of two purposes:

- Find out if she is going to get into bed with you, and/or
- Find out if she is girlfriend material.

If your primary intention is sexual, then you aren't trying to find out much about her nature or if she seems suitable for a long-term relationship. You just want to find out if she is going to take her clothes off with you. In these situations, be reckless, be bold, be sexual – don't worry too much if she would make a good mother for your kids.

On the other hand, if you are more concerned about practicing your dating skills or meeting women who might be good candidates for a long-term relationship, you need to take a completely different approach. We'll talk more about this in later chapters, but in a nutshell, your goal is to create situations where you can find out as much as you can about a woman's nature. A *coffee date* is the ideal way to begin this process.

If you want to explore a woman's nature or practice your dating skills, the initial get-together should always be casual and inexpensive. This creates the optimum way to begin getting to know a woman, while testing for interest and exploring her nature. Contrary to the way most people date, the coffee date is not a time to try and impress your date or get her to like you. It is just a time to meet, check for chemistry, and find out if she is a cool chick.

Doing things to impress a woman or get her to like you is called "seduction." *Seducing someone means you don't believe she could be attracted to you just the way you are.* Unfortunately, this is the way most people date. Doing this is the worst foundation you can lay for a future relationship. The goal of conscious dating is to get to know the woman as she gets to know you, not to seduce each other.

Seduction sets you both up to find out somewhere down the line that you don't really know each other and perhaps don't really like each other. By then, you'll have a bond (and you're probably having sex), which makes it difficult to walk away.

Women can easily fall in love with the process of dating (so can you). Let's say you ask a woman out on a fancy first date – drinks, dinner, a show, dancing. You spend lots of money on her. She gets to go through the pre-date ritual of buying a new outfit and getting her hair and nails done. She tells all her friends about it; before and after. She gets to have a very entertaining weekend night – much more entertaining than sitting home eating frozen pizza and watching a rerun of *Sex and The City*. How will you know if she likes *you* or just the fun dates you provide for her?

Your first date should be simple and inexpensive, with no seduction. You are going to practice skills, test for interest (hers and yours) and find out a little about her nature.

Planning and Paying

You will plan it and you will pay. Since your first date is going to be relatively inexpensive, you can go on lots of first dates without breaking the bank. You pay because it is one way of setting the tone. Paying will also test her nature and tell you how well she follows. Does she offer to pay but allow you to set the tone? Is she gracious? Is she appreciative? If she resists letting you pay for coffee, just tease her a little and hold firm.

If you go on a second date with a woman, pay for this one too. If there is a chemistry developing, she will say something like, "You paid last time, let me get this one." You can say, "No, this one is on me too. If all goes well with this date and you want to see me again, you can plan the next date and I'll let you pay." You are still setting the tone and testing her interest. If she follows up with an invitation for another date, this suggests high interest. If she doesn't ask you out on *her* date, she has low interest – move on.

There are several reasons for meeting the woman at the coffee shop (or wherever) rather than picking her up. The main reason is security. She doesn't know you and probably doesn't want you coming to her home. If she has kids, she doesn't want them to see her picked up by a man they don't know. When the coffee date is over, you can part ways without you having to take her home. The date doesn't get over extended.

On your initial date, get to the location early. By arriving early, you can scope things out, grab a table and make sure it is cleaned off. One former client of mine told me he always shows up late so the woman has to buy her own coffee before he gets there. I kicked his ass! Not the right way to set the tone.

When your date arrives, stand up and wait as she walks toward you. When she gets close, take one step toward her. If it is your first time meeting in person, shake her hand and lightly touch her elbow with your other hand. If you have met before, do the same thing but also lean in and kiss her on the cheek. Greet her, and then invite her to sit down or lead her to the order line. Ask her what she likes, and then order for her.

First Date Basics

I don't want you to memorize the following first date suggestions. Study them though and try practicing three or four of them on your date. Don't try and do it *right*. Remember, it is just practice. As I've stated, you are trying to ascertain the woman's nature and check for interest (yours and hers). If you accomplish these basics, you are doing fine. The rest is just fun and experimentation.

- Be attentive and pay attention to details.
- Make lots of direct eye contact – face-to-face. Don't look around; look at her. As you listen to her talk, move your eyes from her eyes to the top of her forehead and back down to her eyes. Hold for a moment and then do it again. It is okay to look away when you are thinking, but then return to making eye contact again.
- Share things about yourself, but keep it brief. Talk about you for about 45 seconds, then pause and let her share or ask a question.
- Don't be negative or critical.
- Don't talk about exes.
- Ask her questions about herself, but don't interrogate, grill, or interview her. Just be curious about her.
- Make fun of yourself. Tell her about an embarrassing moment.
- Don't try to impress her.

- Test for interest.
- Set the tone and take the lead.

Before the date, think of three questions you want to ask her. This way, you can spend your energy responding to her answers instead of thinking of the next thing you want to know about her – this will keep the conversation going. Remember, most women like to talk. Don't worry about filling the time. Get the ball rolling and she will probably do the rest.

- Get her laughing! Show her your sense of humor. Tease her (at least once).
- Tell her to do something (at least once).
- Lean in and touch her (at least once), just to see how she responds. (Practice the "3 Ts" on every first date. At least once, *tease* her, *touch* her, and *tell* her to do something).
- Breathe, relax your shoulders.
- Smile (but not forced or fake).
- Give yourself permission to make mistakes.
- Imagine the best.
- Be yourself.
- Have fun.

Never bring your date gifts or flowers. You can start doing this after you have been dating a minimum of two months. Guys ask me if it is okay to tell a woman that you think she is pretty or that you like her. The simple answer is: "No!" You can only compliment her in a playful way. "Wow, hot shoes!" "Mmmmm, like that perfume." "Hey, great nails." That's it. Playful and one compliment only. If you had fun, tell her, but only once.

Never ask if you can kiss her, hold her hand, etc. If you have the impulse, just do it.

Be a Gentleman

Practice the following on the first date and on the 300th date. It will never grow old.

- Remember what she likes. When possible, order for her.
- Always open doors and let her enter first.
- Always stand when she enters or leaves the room (in public).
- Always let her be seated first.
- Always open her car door. Always. Tell her to wait for you to open her door – a great way to set the tone AND be a gentleman.
- When walking down a city sidewalk, walk between her and traffic.
- Help her put her coat on and take it off.

Don't be overly obvious about any of these things. Be cool, make it look like second nature.

Practice Being a Good Ender

The initial date should never last longer than an hour. You have something to do at the end of an hour. You end it. If it is going well, leave her wanting more (the first date should never turn into an all-day outing). Have your exit strategy pre-planned: "I'm meeting a friend...," "I'm expecting a call from the east coast...," "I have to let the dog out..."

If you don't plan on seeing her again, walk her to her car, shake her hand, smile, and say something like, "It was nice to meet you, I wish you all the best," or "good luck with your dating." Most people understand this code without having to be so blatant as saying "I'm not going to call again." If she says she would like to see you again, tell her that she is an interesting person but you just don't feel the chemistry. Don't wuss out and tell her that you will call her when you know you won't. This is a great opportunity to practice being a good ender (More on being a good ender in Chapter 19).

If you want to see your date again, walk her to her car and tell her something like, "This was fun. I'll give you a call." Kiss her on the cheek (this is the limit of the physical affection on the first date). The next day, send her a very brief email or text message telling her you enjoyed the date. Don't contact her again for at least three days. Let her ponder for a few days when you will call and what you will have planned. When you call, have a plan for something a little more intriguing than a basic coffee date, but still not a big production. Let it build.

Let's Be Friends

What if you think the date has gone well and you tell her that you are going to call her again and she says she just wants to be friends? This is typically the kiss of death. Bad daters have a tendency of spending way too much time and energy trying to make unavailable women available and unaroused women aroused. They think it is good strategy to be friends with a woman to whom they are attracted, while hoping that someday she will want them in the same way. Don't go there – it is dating suicide. *Women rarely make the leap from platonic friend to wild and crazy sex partner.* This is an example of the woman setting the tone. If she sets the tone from the beginning of whatever relationship you have with her, this will probably never change.

Practice, Practice, Practice

I wrote this chapter while in Sayulita, Mexico, a little coastal town just north of Puerto Vallarta. The beach in Sayulita is known for its great surf, so I decided to take surf lessons while here. After a 15-minute introduction on dry land, I headed into the surf with my board and instructor. Over the course of an hour, I rode about 20 waves. I wiped out on every one.

Most times, I wiped out before I ever really got started. On some attempts, after a few seconds. A couple of times, I felt the exhilaration of riding the waves – for a brief moment or two. But, eventually, I wiped out on every ride.

After each attempt, my instructor gave me something new to try on my next ride. On some waves, I paid attention to pushing up on the board. On others, I thought about where to place my back foot. On some rides I focused on how far up the board to place my front foot. Other times, I worked on staying low with my weight on my front foot. On a couple of rides, it all came together. Most of the time, it didn't.

None of my wipe outs were proof that I am a *failure* or a *loser*. None were proof that I lack the ability to surf. None were proof that surfing is too difficult for me to learn. They were just a predictable part of the learning curve. If you ride enough waves and learn from your failures and your successes, you eventually develop skills that increase your success rate and, subsequently, your confidence level.

Get the analogy?

The 12/12 lets you wipe out over and over again. Each time you do, just go on another date and work on what you learned from the last date. Try out new skills and stretch yourself. Most importantly, have fun. Laugh at yourself (I had the biggest grin on my face after every single wipe out). Get back on the board and try again. You never know which wave will end up giving you the ride of your life!

CHAPTER 14: AVOID THE NUMBER ONE MISTAKE MOST MEN MAKE WITH WOMEN

A woman can't follow where a man doesn't lead.

A while back, I was sitting in the bar of a local restaurant with some men who had taken one of my dating classes. An attractive waitress I know walked by our table. I called her over and asked, "Jessica, how do you like it when the guy you are dating leaves all the decisions up to you and repeatedly asks you what you want to do?"

Without hesitation, Jessica emphatically retorted, "IT IRRITATES ME!" I thanked her for her candid response and turned back to the guys and smiled.

The major mistake that most men and the majority of bad daters make with women is they interact with them passively and force the woman to set the tone and take the lead. 98% of the time, if the man doesn't set the tone and the woman does, she will set a tone for becoming *friends*. Rarely will a woman set the tone for becoming lovers if the man fails to.

In order to avoid falling into the *friend zone*, you have to be willing to get to rejection as quickly as possible. To do this, you have to step up and be bold. You do this by setting the tone and taking the lead. Here is what happens when you set the tone and take the lead in a bold way:

- You stimulate a woman's interest.
- You avoid wasting time on a woman with low interest.

- You project confidence and self-assurance.
- You avoid hearing the dreaded "let's just be friends."

The concept of being bold, setting the tone and taking the lead, and getting to rejection quickly makes all BDs anxious. Doing these things challenges your deepest paradigms about being a good man and about what women want. Though this chapter may make you uncomfortable, it offers a proven model for attracting the attention of women and building healthy long-term relationships, without becoming a girlfriend with a penis.

Leading and Following

I know the concept of leading and following seems almost old fashioned in our "modern" society. Yet someone has to set the tone. No matter how much you hear about equality and 50/50 relationships, cars still come with only one steering wheel and televisions with only one remote. When it comes down to it, someone has to lead.

The golden rule of setting the tone and taking the lead is that you always treat a woman with integrity and respect. Setting the tone and taking the lead is not the same as being controlling, manipulative, selfish, or abusive. This is not about making every decision or having everything go your way. Rather, it is about you *deciding what YOU want and inviting a woman to join you.*

Setting the tone and taking the lead with a woman is like being the lead on a dance floor. A woman has a choice to follow or not. You aren't forcing her to do anything. But she doesn't have a choice if you don't clearly lead or let her know what direction you are going.

Security-Seeking Creatures

Whether you are testing for interest or in an established relationship, you have to set the tone and take the lead. As I have stated in previous chapters, women are by nature, security-seeking creatures, therefore they want to feel safe more than anything else. This is how they are wired. They naturally look to men for *security* (it starts with daddy and continues into adulthood in their intimate relationships with men).

When I talk about a woman's need for *security*, I'm not talking about *money* as most BDs mistakenly assume. *For women, security means not having to guess what a man is thinking or where he wants to go.* Furthermore, it means not having to take responsibility for making all the decisions and not having to take charge. *A healthy woman wants a man who has a plan, who can make decisions, and who can communicate.* If she can't trust the man in her life to make her feel safe, she is forced into taking charge. Women hate this (Jessica was telling the truth)!

All too often, a woman has to take over the man's job by default because the guy won't do it. When a woman takes the lead, the guy assumes she wants to be in charge, even though she doesn't. Once she has gotten behind the wheel, she won't let go unless she is 100% convinced she can trust her man to take over and drive. When a woman is forced into the driver's seat, her sexual interest disappears. This is how a man ends up getting *friended* or *ghosted*.

When a man fails to set the tone and take the lead, the woman:

- Feels unsafe
- Loses trust
- Loses sexual desire
- Has to escalate testing behavior
- Has to become controlling (not a pretty sight)

When a man fails to do his job and forces the woman to set the tone and take the lead, the man becomes:

- Frustrated
- Resentful
- Emotionally unavailable
- Manipulative
- Passive-aggressive
- Moody (also not a pretty sight)

This is why it is essential for you to set the tone and take the lead from the very first moment you meet a woman. These behaviors are the only way to effectively get a woman's attention and keep her interest once you have it. The way you interact with a woman from your very first encounter will determine the way the relationship plays out if it moves forward.

Setting the Tone on The First Date

It is crucial that you set the tone and take the lead before the first date and on the date itself. From the very beginning, be decisive. Tell your date when and where to meet you. Don't give her a bunch of options. Don't force her to make too many decisions. She should only have to decide one thing – is she going to meet you when and where you proposed or not?

I know it may be difficult to sort out how this isn't being controlling, but it isn't. When you take the lead, she has the option to follow or not. She also has the option of offering a counter suggestion. By giving her one choice, you are testing her in such a clear way that her response will be equally clear. When you give a woman too many options or no direction at all ("What would you like to do?"), there is no clear test for her to respond to. All you've really done is frustrate her (remember Jessica's response).

Also, most bad daters can be pretty black and white. They have a tendency to take what I've written above and become rigid and demanding, "Meet me Sunday afternoon at 5:00 PM, or else ….." You don't need an iron fist to set the tone and take the lead – just have a clear plan and invite her to join you!

On the date, you can set the tone by teasing her and making her laugh. Bust on her. Tell her what to do in playful, confident ways. Order for her. Be a gentleman. Tell her to wait until you open her door. Listen. Find out what is important to her. If she starts talking about downer subjects, steer the conversation to lighter fare. You decide when the date ends. Leave her wanting more. Kiss her on the cheek when you tell her goodbye. If she wants to take it further, don't let her. Tease her about wanting to go so fast on a first date. With a wink, tell her you're not that kind of guy.

The whole first date is a test. Think of it just like a game of chess. You are testing her and she is testing you. You are testing to find out as much as you can about her nature and how well she follows. She is testing you to see if you can lead and make her feel safe. One woman I went out with tested me within the first 45 seconds of our date by trying to take control. I lovingly continued to set the tone. She told me later during the same date that she doesn't like it if a man lets her take control. If you passively let a woman set the tone, you have failed her test and she'll lose interest quickly.

Setting the Tone Early in a Relationship

As a new relationship develops, you have to continue setting the tone and taking the lead. I have found that there is a direct correlation between how desperate a guy is and how willing he is to give a woman everything she wants. I have also found that the prettier, sexier, or moodier a woman is, the more likely a man is to let her set the tone. There is also a direct correlation between the degree that a man wants to please a woman and how little respect she will have for him.

Never let a woman dictate the terms of the relationship – ever! As odd as this sounds, letting the woman set the tone is unloving. We tend to think that relationships are the area of feminine expertise, but if you let a woman climb into the driver's seat of the relationship, you'll never get her out and she will quickly lose her attraction to you. Here is why: Because they are security-seeking creatures, *women have a tendency to trade long-term security for short-term gratification* (I know this is a generalization – but test it to see if it holds up).

The feminine (in ourselves and in a woman) wants to feel good RIGHT NOW. This is why she eats chocolate to soothe herself when her jeans don't fit. This is why she buys shoes she doesn't need and charges them on a maxed out credit card when she is stressed about money. Behaving this way helps her feel good in the moment, regardless of the long-term consequences.

If a woman really likes you, she will want to escalate the relationship quickly. This tendency toward emotional fusion tends to be the nature of the feminine. It also tends to be the nature of most BDs. If she likes you, she will want to start talking to you on the phone every night. She will want to text and email. She will want to see you several times a week. She will want to become sexual way too quickly (sometimes on the first or second date).

It is your job to go as slowly as possible to find out as quickly as possible what her nature is. If you get fused and sexual too quickly, you won't get to find out her true nature until somewhere down the line. By then, you will be so bonded that it will be extremely painful for everyone involved if you try to end it. This is why it is your job to set the tone from the very beginning. By doing so, you make the long-term well-being of the relationship (as well as yours and the woman's) a priority over the short-term gratification that both of you want to tumble into.

Chatting

An important rule of setting the tone early in the relationship is *don't chat.* The feminine loves to talk and loves the feeling of having regular contact with a new crush. The average BD loves the feeling too. This is a short-term, *chemical in the brain* gratification. Don't do it. Stay off the phone. Limit emails and text messages in the first few weeks of a new relationship.

If you start chatting on the phone, texting, and emailing right away you are making several mistakes.

- You are letting the woman set the tone.
- You are giving her way too much of what she wants and getting little in return. Early in a relationship, men get little value from chatting on the phone. You can't see her breasts, you can't touch her face, you can't smell her perfume, you can't find out who she really is. Talking is important, but keep those great conversations live and in person.
- Chatting on the phone and emailing early on creates the risk of you becoming her boyfriend way too quickly. It speeds things up and creates an artificial bond.
- You run the risk of becoming a guy friend whom she talks to on the phone but whom she doesn't get naked with!

In the first few weeks of a relationship, the phone and email are for setting up dates, not for chatting. Screen all calls. *If she calls you, let it go to voicemail.* Wait a little while before calling her. When you do call her, simply make plans to see each other in person. I know this sounds like game playing, but it is essential for setting a healthy tone in the relationship.

Keep on Setting the Tone

As a relationship unfolds, continue to set the tone and take the lead:

- Never allow a woman to tell you that you can't see your friends or can't spend time enjoying your hobbies.
- Don't engage in conversations you don't want to have.
- Don't argue and don't try to convince her of anything.
- *Never, ever, ever defend yourself – it makes you feel and appear weak.*
- Never let her treat you badly. Be willing to walk away.

Remember, there are boatloads of great women out there. When you let a woman treat you badly or when you put up with something that you don't like, the tone has been established for the rest of the relationship.

Letting go of Attachment to Outcome

The Buddha said that *attachment is the cause of all suffering.* Attachment is also the cause of all bad dating. In order to set the tone and take the lead, you have to work at letting go of attachment to outcome. If you are worried about outcomes you will never take a risk, test for interest, blurt, ask a woman out, get a phone number, initiate sex, or set the tone in a relationship.

Letting go of attachment to outcome is a mental process.

- Tell yourself a woman's response is never personal.
- Tell yourself "No matter what happens, I can handle it."
- Breathe, have fun, be willing to make a mistake.
- Be willing to look foolish.
- Learn to laugh at yourself.
- Treat dating as research.
- See all interactions as an adventure.

Letting go of attachment to outcome allows you to lean into your fear of rejection. If you aren't attached to outcomes, rejection doesn't hurt. But, if you internalize that a woman's low interest means you are undesirable and unlovable and that every woman will feel the same, yes, you will *make yourself* pretty miserable. But, the actual low interest response – the *rejection*, if you will – doesn't hurt.

I suggested in an earlier chapter that you go out and try to get rejected three times in an evening. As I wrote, I've discovered something really powerful about trying to get rejected. The guys who go out and do the assignment experience amazing growth. They begin to have unbelievable success in their dating experience. The guys who never try to get rejected also never seem to make much progress in their dating or mating.

This is true for a least a couple of reasons. One is that if you approach women trying *not* to get rejected, you will be passive and indirect. Women will pick up on this. On the other hand, approaching women and trying to get them to reject you makes you seem bold and confident. Even women who aren't available find this energy attractive.

The second reason this assignment is so powerful is that when you *try* to get rejected, your anxiety level actually starts going down. The more your anxiety goes down, the more likely you are to interact with women, test for interest, and set the tone and take the lead. This creates a positive feedback loop. As you feel more confident, you approach more women. And, when you approach more women, you feel more confident.

As you let go of attachment to outcome and try to get rejected, you will be able to test, set the tone, and take the lead more effectively. Women will be attracted to your confidence and masculine strength. They will feel secure and aroused.

By letting go of attachment to outcome, getting rejected starts to feel like a game. I've gone out some nights with the goal of getting rejected five times before the night was over. Not only did I have a surprising amount of fun, but I also interacted with women I normally wouldn't have. I've had so much success at times that I've never actually gotten five rejections!

CHAPTER 15: LEARN AND PRACTICE THE SECRETS OF NATURAL PLAYERS

Most men quit testing before a woman quits showing high interest.

When I started dating in my late forties, I had no idea how to find out if a woman liked me or how to tell if she was in a relationship. I had no clue how or when to ask for her phone number, or whether or not to ask her out. I assumed that all of these things required lots of luck, E.S.P., or some skill that my parents just didn't pass on to me.

- Did I read that right? Was she flirting or just being friendly?
- She doesn't have a ring on, but what if I come on to her and find out she is in a relationship?
- What if I ask her out and she says no. I'll look foolish.

As a result, I felt unsure about how to interact with women. Therefore, I typically did nothing. If I did engage, I did it indirectly, subtly, and ineffectively.

In my research on dating skills, I came across the concept of *testing for interest* and I began experimenting with women I met. Before long, all of the questions and doubts I previously had about approaching women began to fade. Most importantly, once I developed an understanding of how to test, interacting with women became unbelievably easy!

Every time I teach the concept of testing for interest to men, their response is always something like, "That's simple, I can do that!" If you have been a bad dater all of your life, I know this sounds impossible.

But I promise you, once you understand how to test for interest, you will transform into a man who can get phone numbers within minutes – and do it several times in an evening. I am still amazed at how easy it is once you know what you are doing.

The Secret

The secret of testing for interest is simply this:

- Every interaction you have with a woman is a test of her interest in interacting with you.
- Testing has only one purpose – to check for interest level (i.e., a person's interest in having an interaction with you).
- A woman either has high interest or low interest in interacting with you. That is all you have to find out.
- A woman's response isn't personal. If a woman responds with low interest, you don't have to figure out why, it doesn't matter.
- Testing tends to raise a woman's interest level.
- Testing allows you to get to rejection quickly. You don't waste time and money. Nor do you miss out on the opportunity to test other women who might have higher interest.
- There is no middle ground. A woman has either high or low interest in interacting with you (don't make this complicated).

It's that simple. No mind reading, no guessing, nothing else to figure out. When you test a woman for interest, you are not trying to find out if she likes you. You are not giving her the power to accept or "reject" you. Therefore, whenever you approach a woman, talk to a woman, flirt with a woman, or tell a woman to give you her number – you only have to pay attention to one thing – her interest level. She either has high interest or low interest in interacting with you. That's it.

If she says, "I have a boyfriend," or "I'm busy all next week," or "I don't give out my number," you don't have to figure out if any of these statements are true. You don't have to feel rejected or take her low interest personally. You don't have to figure out why she has low interest. You don't have to vilify her. You just smile, move on, and test another woman.

It is such a relief to be able to:

- Let go of trying to figure out how to say *the right thing* to a woman
- Not have to try and read a woman's mind
- Not have to figure out why a woman does what she does
- Not worry if a woman likes you
- Not guess if a woman is in a relationship
- Not take anything a woman does personally
- Have a tool that raises the likelihood of succeeding with women

Three Levels of Testing

Testing for interest occurs primarily at three levels. Without being aware of it, you have probably followed this social model many times in many situations. Countless other people have used it on you to test your interest in interacting with them. Once you clearly understand the model, you will see that it is the basis of pretty much all social interaction. When you really understand how testing for interest works, you will find your social skills, social intelligence, and confidence growing by leaps and bounds. At the end of this chapter you will say, "Oh, that's simple. Why didn't anyone ever show me how to do it that way before?"

In all of my *Dating Essentials for Men* podcasts, courses, and seminars, I strongly encourage men to get out of the house, expand their route, and talk to people everywhere they go. You probably didn't realize it, but this is the most basic form of testing. You should be testing everyone you meet – men and women, young and old (note: do not take this literally – you don't have to talk to everyone you meet during your day, but do take advantage of opportunities to talk to new people).

This practice not only makes the world a friendlier place, but it also opens doors to creating new relationships, business opportunities, and dates. The information that follows primarily focuses on women, but the principles can be applied to all social situations.

Please note, you can't wait until you meet a woman you find attractive to decide to start practicing your testing skills. You have to practice your testing skills every day with everyone you meet. Otherwise, when you do meet a woman you want to test, you will feel awkward, anxious, and unsure. I call this daily testing, *playing in the minors*. In all the history of Major League Baseball, only a handful of players were naturally gifted enough to skip the minor leagues altogether and go right to the majors. Even the most talented athletes typically spend years hitting minor league pitching before they can successfully take a cut at a major league fastball or slider.

The same principle applies to you. Your "minor league" is the people you meet day in and day out in the elevator, at the coffee shop, on the bus, or at the gym. That is why you have to get out of the house, expand your route, linger in public, and talk to people everywhere you go. It is all practice.

Your "major league" will be the attractive woman standing in line next to you at the coffee shop. Since you will already have developed the habit of testing everyone you meet, you will just do with her what you have already been doing with everyone else. You will feel relaxed, confident, and engaging. All those cuts you took in the minors will pay off as you swing for the fences with a major league woman.

Level One Testing: Social Pleasantries

Level One testing consists of the most basic social interactions like smiling, making and maintaining eye contact, saying hello, commenting on the weather, etc. I have found that most BDs typically don't initiate these basic social pleasantries. They are afraid of intruding, being inappropriate, or looking foolish. But basic social pleasantries are where testing begins, and they are the foundation of all other testing.

Most BDs make Level One testing way too difficult and way too overwhelming. This isn't rocket science. Be like a child with no social filters or inhibitions. Just smile, say hello, make any random comment to people with whom you come into contact. These Level One tests can include:

- Commenting on anything in your environment – "Think it will ever stop raining?" "Wow, they're really busy here today."
- Asking how a person is doing – "How's your day going so far?" "Enjoying the sunshine?"

- Something you observe about a person or the situation – "Have a good workout?" "Been shopping?"
- An open-ended or opinion question – In a restaurant, "What's good here?" While standing in a checkout line looking at a tabloid, "Think Brad will ever get back with Angelina?"
- A person's name – "Hey, what's your name?" Practice remembering people's names. Repeat them and use them in conversation. If you forget someone's name, ask again.

I suggest you don't use "Hi" as a Level One test. There is nothing for the person to respond to or engage with – there is no real test. My tried-and-true Level One test is simply, "How's your day going so far?"

I know that this all probably sounds overly simplistic and you might even wonder what it has to do with dating (on the other hand, I know those of you with high social anxiety are already quaking). You don't need clever pickup lines or contrived *sets* to start a conversation with a woman. Simple is better.

To illustrate this assertion, several years ago I was in a hot nightclub in Scottsdale, AZ. Two women came over and stood near me. I asked them, "What's the worst pickup line you've heard tonight?" One of them laughed and said, "That one." I smiled back and asked, "What's the best one?" The other woman replied, "You don't need a pickup line, just introduce yourself."

High vs. Low Interest

Remember, *at all three levels of testing, you only have to observe one thing – the person's apparent interest in interacting with you.* That's it. You don't have to figure out if you are intruding, if you've said the wrong thing, or if they like you. People will demonstrate either high interest or low interest when interacting with you. There is nothing else to figure out and nothing else in between.

What does high interest look like? You say, "How do you like that book?" She smiles and says, "It's great, I really love this author. Have you read anything by her?" Her facial expressions, body language, and voice tone are all open and welcoming. She engages you.

What does low interest look like? You say, "What's good here?" She says, "I don't know," and looks away.

Pretty simple, isn't it!

If a woman shows low interest, don't take it personally. Don't get discouraged. Don't apologize. Don't try and figure out what you did wrong. Don't try and figure out why she has low interest. Don't project negative or evil intent on her. Don't try and figure anything out. Don't assume that every other woman will feel just like her. She just has low interest. Smile and move on.

Many BDs express the fear of intruding on strangers or being the bore who doesn't "get it" – you know, the guy sitting next to you on the airplane going on and on about his bad back for hours, not noticing that everyone around him would rather be poking a sharp stick in their ears. You never run the risk of being a nuisance when you are testing because you are observing a person's response to each test. As soon as they show low interest, you smile and move on. This is what people with natural social intelligence do.

How do you tell if a person has high interest or if they're just being friendly and polite? Easy. The conversation will naturally move to Level Two.

Level Two Testing: Finding Commonality

Level Two testing is organic. You don't have to make it happen, you just have to go with it when it happens on its own.

At Level Two, you are testing for *mutual high interest*. You are measuring your interest in a woman, as well as her interest in you. Level Two testing allows you to get to know more about a woman and gives her the chance to get to know you. You are exploring to see if a woman is someone you might want to ask out or have sex with.

Level Two testing gives you a chance to explore a woman's nature. You are testing for sense of humor and flexibility. You are gauging her intelligence and awareness of cultural and social issues. You are exploring common interests. You are looking to see if she is playful, passionate, and comfortable with physical touch. You are assessing her personal beliefs, values, and morals. You are finding out if she is a cool chick.

Many men tell me that they aren't good at small talk and therefore believe that women won't find them interesting. Here's the good news: Most women like to talk! If they have high interest, they will do most of the heavy lifting for you!

You don't have to be a great conversationalist to test for interest. You just have to do *something* (what you say usually isn't even all that important). If the woman has any kind of interest in you, she will carry the bulk of the conversation. If a woman doesn't say much to you there are usually one of two reasons: She is shy (and not good at small talk) or she has low interest. So, if you test for interest and the conversation quickly dies, don't assume you did something wrong or lack skills. Assume she is shy or has low interest. You found out exactly what you want to know!

At Level Two, you can tease her, discuss commonalities, ask opinion questions, state your point of view, bust on her, shift from serious to playful, make deals, or say off the wall things. *The only goal of testing is to measure interest (yours and hers).* Never try to impress her and don't try to get her to like you. Don't buy her drinks (this does absolutely nothing to test a woman's interest and makes you look like a doormat).

Level Two testing also gives you an effective way to find out if a woman is in a relationship. Women usually let you know (often in code) during a Level Two interaction if they are with someone. They sense that the conversation has moved from Level One – social pleasantries – to Level Two (women just seem to get these things). They want to be friendly, but they also want to help you avoid an embarrassing social blunder.

At some point during a Level Two conversation she will mention her husband, kids, or boyfriend in a casual way, "We took the kids to Hawaii this summer," or "My boyfriend is a big Yankees fan too." Some guys take this personally, but it is actually an example of the woman doing the considerate thing and treating you with respect. Take the hint and enjoy the conversation for what it is.

As your Level Two testing unfolds, you can observe her signs of high interest – lingering, flirting, eye contact, smiles, asking you questions, touching you, laughing at your jokes (probably one of the highest signs of interest from a woman), suggestive comments, moving toward you, talking to her friends about you, inviting you to join her in some activity.

As conversation flows and heats up, more advanced Level Two tests can include physical contact – moving closer to her, leaning in and out (this "push/pull" or "lean" is a fundamental part of flirting and testing), touching her arm or the small of her back, whispering in her ear, touching some accessory she is wearing, taking her hand, kissing her cheek. All of these physical actions and her response to them give you a gauge of her interest.

If a woman responds with repeated high interest to your tests at Level Two (this may take anywhere from a few seconds to a few minutes), and you have interest in her, move to Level Three.

Level Three Testing: Require Something of Her

Level Three is where most guys (not just BDs) falter. Things have been going well. You've been having a lively conversation. She has laughed at your jokes. You seem to have a lot in common. You'd like to see her again. But because Level Three is where the greatest chance for rejection comes, most guys chicken out and miss out on a great opportunity.

Most men quit testing before a woman quits showing high interest!

Once you get to Level Three, the odds are high that something really interesting is going to happen as a result of your testing. Be prepared for the response. Level Three is where you test for the whole enchilada. This is where you take things to the next level and find out how far they can go.

One of the biggest complaints I hear from women is that men will be friendly but not ask for a number or set up a date. This frustrates women to no end because most don't want to come across as too aggressive. It is your job to close the deal. It is your job to make the ultimate test for interest. Going for the close can be scary – but you've gotten this far, so the odds are great you'll get a high interest response to your Level Three test.

This is the beauty of understanding and using the three levels of testing. She has already shown high interest at Level One. She has already shown high interest at Level Two. You have already gotten her to "yes" several times. She is primed and interested. She is just waiting for you to take it to the next level. Don't let her down. Open the door for her to walk through.

Here is the primary way Level Three testing differs from Levels One and Two: *Testing at Level Three involves requiring the woman do something.* Requiring something of a woman is the ultimate test of interest. Telling her to do something allows you to get to rejection quickly. You'll find out if she truly has high interest or if she is just enjoying a pleasant conversation with you.

The two most common and socially acceptable ways to test a woman for interest at Level Three are to get a phone number or tell a woman to meet you for a specific event at a specific time. Both are powerful because you are requiring a strong commitment from her. These two tests are not meant so much to get a number or set up a meeting as they are to test her interest. Your goal is to see how high her interest is, and then possibly drive it up higher.

Every Day, Everywhere You Go

The following chapters in this book will give you specific strategies and techniques for testing women. Remember, it is much easier than you think and the results will prove to be amazing.

I like testing for interest because it's organic and it works. This process is a reflection of everyday social interaction. Consciously testing for interest raises your social IQ in all kinds of life situations. It isn't contrived and it doesn't involve memorizing a bunch of canned routines. It isn't manipulative or phony. Testing for interest doesn't turn you into a geek with techniques or some #MeToo casualty tale.

While this chapter has primarily been about how to test women for interest, the principles apply to all people in all situations. Test men, women, old people, young people, attractive people and unattractive people. *Remember, if you wait until you see a woman you find attractive to practice testing, you won't do anything or you will do something BADLY!*

Get out of the house and talk to people everywhere you go. Test, test, test. Practice, practice, practice. Most importantly, have fun!

CHAPTER 16: YOU'VE GOT HER ATTENTION, NOW DRIVE UP HER INTEREST

Make a bold gesture of the lusty type.

In the previous chapter, I presented the three levels of testing that natural players use to find out if a woman is interested and available. This kind of testing is the most effective way to find out how interested a woman is in interacting with you, if she is already in a relationship, and when to close. But testing is even more than that. *Testing for interest is the most effective way to get a woman's attention and boost her interest level.*

I have experienced numerous situations where women hadn't even noticed me until I began testing them. As I tested, their interest level rose from non-existent to very high in just a matter of moments. Their interest didn't go up because she noticed how good looking I am, how nice a car I drive, or how great my ass looks in my jeans. Their interest went up because I tested them.

The more a woman responds to your tests, the more her interest level goes up. This is true for several reasons:

- Testing inserts you into her consciousness. If she doesn't know you exist or hasn't noticed you, she can't possibly have high interest in you.
- Every time she responds positively to one of your tests, her mind convinces her that you must be an interesting guy. Otherwise, she

wouldn't be responding positively to your tests – her mind has to rationalize her behavior. This is called *high perceived value.*

- Testing projects confidence more effectively than anything else I know. Since confidence is one of the most powerful aphrodisiacs for women, testing for interest is the best way to get a woman's attention and keep it.
- Testing creates something I call *positive emotional tension* (PET). Women need emotional tension for attraction and attachment.

Be Bold

To be effective, testing has to be bold. You can't be passive or subtle. Unless your test is bold, a woman can't give you a clear answer. *Every test has to be so clear that the woman's response to it is equally clear.*

The biggest mistake you can make, especially at Level Three, is to be too subtle or indirect. The typical *nice* way of asking a woman out not only fails to gauge or drive up her interest, it also forces the woman to figure out exactly what it is you are asking.

- Are you busy next weekend? (she doesn't know what you have in mind)
- Maybe we should go out sometime (vague and wimpy)
- If I were to ask you out, would you say 'yes?' (my old standard)
- It was nice to meet you, have a good day (crash and burn)

You have to be willing to risk being told "no." You have to lean into the fear of rejection. If the woman already has interest in you, this boldness will drive her interest up even more. Remember, your goal is to get to rejection as quickly as possible.

You have to give her the chance to tell you "no." Level Three testing allows you to do this effectively and quickly. Once you know a woman has low interest, you can move on and find a woman who has high interest. If you can't test effectively, you'll end up spending way too much time with the wrong woman – and not know it.

Remember, as I stressed in the previous chapter, in order to test boldly and clearly *you have to let go of all attachment to outcome.* Any agenda on your part will invalidate the test. As soon as you start caring about outcomes, you are no longer testing effectively. Attachment to outcome will make you *risk averse.*

Effective testing requires risk. If you interact with a woman thinking, "I hope she likes me," or "I hope she doesn't reject me," your testing will lose its effectiveness. Why? Because you will seem needy and timid, as opposed to assured and confident. Your agenda will get in the way of how clearly you test and how accurately you read her response.

Don't worry about the outcome. Don't worry how she feels about your testing. If a person responds with low interest, it doesn't mean there is something wrong with you or that you did something wrong. One woman's low interest is not an indicator that all women will have low interest.

Let things go where they go.

- If she has high interest – *GREAT!*
- If she has low interest – *GREAT!*

Learn to become equally okay with either outcome.

Getting Unstuck at Level Three

Here's an important point: *Needing a woman's approval is the biggest hindrance to moving from Level Two testing to Level Three testing.*

A lot of guys tell me that they get good at Level One and Level Two testing, but seem to get hung up on Level Three testing. They'll tell me about good conversations they have with a woman. Everything goes well. The woman sends them good vibes. But when it is time to move to Level Three and require something of her, they freeze. They end up walking away and kicking themselves for not pulling the trigger. These guys repeatedly get stuck at Level Two.

Here is what is happening: *These men are attached to getting a woman's approval.* Once they have her approval at Levels One and Two, they don't want to do anything that might risk losing it. This need for feminine approval is so strong, these men will walk away from an interested woman because they are afraid of doing anything that might cause her to think less of them.

Moving to Level Three always involves risk. If you need women to always approve of you – or put another way – if you are terrified of having a woman disapprove of you, you will probably never do what it takes to really test for interest. To be successful at testing, you have to let go of your attachment to women's approval. *The need for feminine approval is actually what has kept you from getting the love and sex you want.*

Testing for interest everywhere you go is a great way to practice letting go of your need for universal approval, especially the approval of women. Not every woman is going to approve of you, and that's okay. You don't need women to approve of you. If you are willing to risk the loss of a few women thinking you are a great guy, you actually open the door to getting to know some really great women.

Again, most men quit testing before women quit showing high interest. Don't be one of those guys. As long as a woman is showing high interest, keep testing. Give her the chance to tell you "no." But more importantly, give her the chance to tell you "YES!"

Revisiting Core Principles

Okay, let's review a few principles presented in previous chapters in the context of testing for interest. As I've stated, confidence is a huge turn-on for women. Bold testing projects confidence. There are some very specific things you can do as you progress through the levels of testing to make you look even more confident.

Set the tone and take the lead.

BDs have a hard time with this one because they don't want to be controlling. They want to be the perfect gentleman. If this is true for you, you probably believe that letting the woman set the tone is respectful. Perhaps your mother taught you to be respectful to women, your father didn't treat your mother well, or you've listened to too many women complain about the *jerks* who treat them badly. Whatever the case – you've come to believe that showing women the traits that project confidence will make you appear like a *bad man*. This is your own internal SLB. Women love a confident man with a plan.

Take the risk.

Women will see your bold initiative as confidence. Women don't want to be burdened with making decisions about where the relationship goes. They want you to have a plan and present it with style and enthusiasm. Not only does this project confidence, it is also a great test for whether or not the woman will follow (and it shows you how high her interest is).

Tell her what to do.

Telling a woman what to do may seem not *nice*, but as we've discussed in previous chapters, women are not turned on by *nice*. *Telling her to do what she already wants to do* ratchets up her interest in you, shows her you are a leader, and projects a hell of a lot of confidence.

Being assertive isn't controlling, it is giving her an option. Tell her to meet you somewhere, "Meet me tomorrow at 4:00 at Joe's for happy hour." Tell her what to do, "Buy me a drink," "Order for me," "Rub my neck, it's really sore." Tell her what to do without even speaking a word. Point to your cheek and lean toward her (expecting a kiss). Grab her hand and lead her somewhere.

Obey the Three-Second Rule.

Whenever you see a woman or group of women you want to meet, don't hesitate. Move in and test immediately. This projects confidence. Every time you hesitate longer than three seconds, you give your mind a chance to think too much *(Remember: thinking causes anxiety, acting cures it)*. Your anxiety will skyrocket and either you won't approach and test, or you will do so clumsily. By following the *Three-Second Rule,* you will always approach without hesitation and say the first thing that comes to mind. What comes out of your mouth will be fresh, spontaneous and engaging. You will look confident.

Get her number.

If you have received high interest at Levels One and Two, and want to get a phone number, take out your mobile phone and say, "Give me your number." Tell her, "I'm going to call you and set a time to continue our conversation." Key her number in and push call. Give it a chance to ring.

"There, I've got your number and you've got mine." Later, enter her name to go along with her number.

When She Doesn't Seem to Show High Interest at Level Three

Sometimes a woman will appear to show high interest at Levels One and Level Two, but when you test at Level Three, she responds with low interest. This can be confusing, but don't try to figure it out.

- Some women enjoy male attention and flirting even if they aren't interested in developing a relationship (or aren't available for one).
- Sometimes a woman just doesn't walk through the door you have opened.
- Sometimes a woman is afraid or just hasn't talked herself into it yet.

There's no way to know, and it doesn't matter. If a woman has shown high interest at the first two levels of testing but seemingly low interest at Level Three, it doesn't hurt to try one more test. Sometimes, she just needs one more opportunity to walk through the door. Maybe your test hasn't been bold enough.

Weak Tests

A college-aged client of mine asked me about a situation in which one of his female friends from high school had been acting more friendly than usual. He was attracted to her and wondered how he could test her interest. I suggested he set up a coffee date with her. When she entered the coffee shop, I told him to walk toward her, put his hand on the small of her back, firmly and confidently pull her toward him, and give her a kiss on the lips.

He exclaimed, "Oh no, what if she goes ballistic?" He told me that he was thinking about sending her flowers to test her interest. I explained that she wouldn't go ballistic if he kissed her and that sending flowers isn't a test – it doesn't require anything of the woman. The only way he could really assess her true interest level was to take the lead and see if she followed.

Another client told me that he had been on five dates with a woman. She kept going out with him but never showed any affection. He wondered if she was interested in him or just interested in the dates he took her on. I asked him if he had tested her. He told me that on their last date, he put his hand lightly on her back while walking down the street. I told him this wasn't an effective test, because she had no idea what his touch meant. Nothing was required of her. I suggested that on their next date, while walking down the street, he turn to her and say, "Oh, I almost forgot....." Then, put his arm around her waist, pull her in, and give her a deep kiss. Her response would tell him everything he needed to know.

All of the practices above make you look confident even when you don't feel confident. I'll say it again because it is worth repeating: *Confidence – not looks, money, or penis size – is the number one aphrodisiac for women!* When you boldly test at Level Three – when you require something of a woman – you project confidence!

Remember: When a man projects confidence, a woman experiences the same kind of chemical reaction in her brain that a man experiences when a woman lifts her shirt and shows him her breasts. Even if she isn't available or you aren't her type, she will still feel the "buzz." It's biological. Use this evolutionary response in your favor.

Don't Take Anything a Woman Does Personally

Testing and letting go of attachment will help you get over taking a woman's low interest personally. Nothing a woman does is personal. Whatever her response may be, it is about her, not you. Think about it. You come into contact with numerous women throughout the course of the week. You don't have high interest in every woman you meet. This doesn't mean you are *rejecting* them or you think they are worthless human beings. Your low interest is telling a story about you, not them, because many other men might have high interest in the same women.

Reverse this logic. Just because one individual woman shows low interest in you, that doesn't mean she is *rejecting* you or that you are a worthless human being. It isn't personal. Her low interest doesn't mean that all women will have low interest in you. It doesn't mean that she might not have high interest in you on another day. This is just a reality of life.

Here is a simple illustration: You walk into a pizza place that has five or six kinds of pizza already cooked behind the counter. You pick the kind you want and they heat a slice for you. In that moment, your brain expresses high interest in one kind of pizza (perhaps pepperoni) and lower interest in all the other kinds on display. This doesn't mean that you dislike the other kinds. This doesn't mean that on another day, you might not have high interest in the vegetarian pizza and low interest in the pepperoni. It isn't about the pizza, it is about you. Who knows why you choose one kind one day and another kind another day? There is no need to figure it out. It just is.

The same principles apply to personal attraction. A person's response to you can change from day to day, week to week. It can't be figured out and it isn't personal.

Outs – How to Save Face

Most guys won't test and take risks if they are worried about negative outcomes. Letting go of attachment to outcome helps. In fact, the more you test, the less you'll be affected by low interest responses. They become a part of everyday life. Not to mention that this practice will also open you up to take risks in other areas of life.

I have found that early on, having some pre-prepared, face-saving *outs* can be helpful in pushing through the initial anxiety that comes with testing. These outs are what you fall back on if you get a low interest response. If you get a low interest response at Level One, you typically don't have to do anything. At Level Two, just smile and say, "Have a nice day."

At Level Three, where the test requires a response from the woman, outs can be helpful. If you boldly test and get a low interest response, your outs ensure that you aren't left standing there looking foolish with your tail between your legs. Your outs will give you more confidence to take risks. Some possible Level Three outs might include (say them confidently with a smile):

- You can't blame a guy for trying.
- Take it as a compliment.
- That's okay, when you drop your boyfriend next week, give me a call.
- Don't worry, I won't tell your husband if you don't.
- You won't be able to get me out of your head.

Even your outs will project confidence. They might even raise her interest level to the point where she decides to connect with you after all (I've had that happen).

Walk through the open door!

As long as you are getting high interest responses, don't stop testing. As I've said, The biggest mistake most guy's make is that they quit testing long before a woman stops showing high interest. Since testing raises a woman's interest level, ongoing testing has the power to take interactions to unimaginable levels.

Level Three testing continues even after the initial encounter. If you meet up and continue to see each other, you need to continue to set the tone and take the lead. She may playfully object to you telling her what to do, even as she follows your directions. As soon as you get passive and start asking her what she wants to do, her interest level will wane quickly.

Remember, tell her to do what she already wants to do. Do it playfully and do it with love. You will take her places she has never been and open her up in ways that she never imagined possible. She will thank you for being such a powerful man!

CHAPTER 17: BANTER AND FLIRT LIKE A PRO (EVEN IF YOU'RE SHY OR INTROVERTED)

Relax, take the lid off, and let the real you come out.

I frequently hear men in my *Dating Essentials for Men* programs say things like:

"I don't know how to talk to a **woman**."

"I don't know what to say."

"I'm not funny."

"I'm not interesting."

What these guys are really saying is that they don't know how to banter and flirt. Learning these skills is easier than you think. And, they will supercharge your dating experience. They are exceptional tools for testing for a woman's interest, and a **great** way of communicating your own interest.

Both bantering and flirting are primarily the manifestation of a mental attitude. These behaviors demonstrate confidence – *they show your social IQ, your intelligence, and your comfort with your sexuality.* This combination of traits is a powerful turn-on for the female mind. By demonstrating your fun, playful, and sensual side, it is easier to get a woman to play along with you.

We could probably split hairs over exactly what bantering and flirting are, but I define *banter* as *a playful verbal repartee.* Bantering can be done in many contexts with both men and women. *It is when you add sexual energy to banter that you get flirting.*

If you have high sexual interest in a woman, flirting is a great way to test her sexual interest and drive it up. Since playfulness and comfort with one's sexuality are key ingredients for great sex, it is good to find out if the woman you are testing is comfortable with these aspects of herself.

Many bad daters don't banter or flirt well because it makes them feel vulnerable. They don't want to risk rejection, they are afraid of sex, and/ or they are afraid of women. Some BDs don't grasp innuendo, humor, or subtle social cues well.

You don't have to banter or flirt to get a woman's attention and drive up her interest, but it helps. The more comfortable and adept you become with bantering and flirting, the more opportunity you will have to connect quickly with a greater number of women. Even if you're not a natural, I am convinced you can learn how to banter and flirt better. This chapter will teach you how.

Create a Feeling

Always remember, attraction for a woman is primarily determined by how she feels with a man. Therefore, bantering and flirting are an ideal way to create a positive feeling state. You aren't trying to impress her, make her like you, or draw attention to yourself. Your goal is to test for interest and drive it up. When you do this, you are helping her have fun, while inviting her into your world where she can have a better time than she was having before she met you.

Bantering and flirting are all about being yourself. They aren't about putting on a show. You are inviting a woman to get to know you. You don't have to be clever and you don't have to entertain her. Bantering and flirting allow a woman to see the cool you that isn't wrapped up in worry, anxiety, and self-doubt. You just have to relax, take the lid off, and let the real you come out.

To banter and flirt successfully, you have to get out of your head. Most BDs live inside their *thinker* and are always obsessing about themselves. They worry about looking foolish or anxious. They fret about not saying or doing the right thing. They obsess about what might go wrong. They worry way too much about what people will think of them.

STOP!

Stop worrying. The experts claim that when a woman meets you, only seven percent of her initial impression of you is based on what you say. The other 93 percent is based on your appearance and body language. This is where attitude comes in – just say something! When you walk into a room, own it. Tell yourself that you are "The Man," and that women want to get to know you. It makes more sense to present that kind of image than the one you present when you are spinning in your head consumed with anxiety and self-doubt. Stop worrying. Present the very best YOU! – the smart, affectionate, funny YOU!

Most BDs have some degree of social anxiety. *Talking to an attractive woman ratchets up every man's anxiety.* That is why you can't wait until you see an attractive woman to figure out how you are going to test, banter, or flirt. You should already be doing it every day with everyone you meet. Practice bantering with servers, baristas, grandmas, and little children. This daily practice will help you be more relaxed. Your interactions will be a lot more enjoyable for you and the woman!

Successful bantering and flirting require that you see yourself as a fun person. If you think you are boring and have no clue how to have fun, this will come across to women, even if you have memorized 50 funny or clever things to say. If you think you are dull, start working on yourself. Get whatever help you need to find out how to have fun, not just so you can attract women, but so you can start enjoying life!

Ready to get started? The following pages are chock-full of ideas for bantering and flirting. Don't think you have to use them all. Pick an idea or two and adapt it to your personality. Don't try and memorize a bunch of lines or techniques. It won't be you. Go out and test and play and have a good time.

Remember, most BDs quit testing before a woman has quit showing high interest – don't make that mistake. Bantering and flirting are such powerful ways to test for interest that the results might initially frighten you. You will be amazed how far things can go in a short amount of time when you banter and flirt and don't quit testing until you get to "no."

Bantering and Flirting Basics

Make Eye Contact

Your eyes are transmitters of high interest. Looking directly into the eyes of another person is such a powerful, emotionally loaded act of communication that we normally restrict it to very brief glances. Prolonged eye contact between two people indicates intense emotion and/or intimacy.

Eye contact a is great first level test. When you are in a public place, look around. Check people out. If a woman notices your look, look her in the eye and hold your look for just a moment longer than you're comfortable with. Look away (confidently, as if you have something else important to look at), then look back again and smile. If she holds your gaze, smiles, or sends other indicators of interest, approach her.

It is important that you don't stare or leer at a woman or her body parts. It is creepy. Make the kind of playful, confident eye contact that you would want a woman to make with you.

Blurt

Like many BDs, you might claim that you can't think of anything to say when you approach a woman. You may not believe that you are funny or clever. These SLBs probably are not true. I would bet that you do think of lots of funny or clever things in the moment (or soon after). Unfortunately, you have been trained to filter and sensor what you think. You don't want to say anything stupid, you don't want to look silly or foolish, or you don't want to have something used against you later.

Practice blurting. *Say the things that come to mind without filtering or editing.* Sometimes, it will be funny and unexpected. Sometimes it will be off the wall or inappropriate. That's okay. If a woman has high interest in you, you have to work pretty hard to kill her interest. On the other hand, not saying anything will almost guarantee a total lack of interest from women.

For example, a member of one of my classes was shopping during the holidays at a small store in the mall. The woman ringing up his purchase asked for his phone number as part of the transaction. Without thinking he blurted, "You just want my number so you can call me and ask me out on a date." She blushed and he immediately felt a sense of panic for making such a bold assertion. After a brief moment, the woman replied, "I get off work at 5:00."

Touch

When you banter and flirt, touch is essential. Touch is one of the things that sets the tone and distinguishes the interaction from a dry, impersonal conversation about the weather.

As a general rule, the arm is the safest place to touch a woman you don't know well. A brief arm touch should prompt some reciprocal increase in intimacy if a woman has high interest. If she has low interest, it will show in her physical response and lack of reciprocity. If you see signs of a positive reaction to your arm touch, touch her arm again and maintain your touch. If this results in a further escalation of interest level, move from touching her arm to the small of her back, her hair, her face, her leg. If she has high interest, each touch makes her feel special and ratchets up her interest even more. Do this casually and confidently as if it were natural and spontaneous.

If you seem to receive low interest responses when you touch a woman, lean back a little. Don't try and force anything. You aren't trying to make anything happen, you are leading to see if she follows. If she doesn't, great. Respect her space.

Reciprocal Disclosure

One of the most important aspects of bantering and flirting is what psychologists call *reciprocal disclosure* – the exchange of personal information. When you first meet, these details do not have to be particularly intimate. They can even be humorous or nonsensical. If a woman discloses information about herself, reciprocate by revealing some similar information about yourself, perhaps raising the ante with something slightly more personal ("I sucked my thumb until kindergarten"). If she has high interest, she will probably try to match your disclosure with one of similar value.

Play the "Shy Card"

If you are shy and it makes you anxious to interact with women, use that to your advantage. Approach her and tell her that you are really shy but you knew that if you didn't walk over and introduce yourself, you'd kick yourself later. Tell her you are not good at pickup lines. Focus on her rather than your shyness and she will see you as courageous for challenging yourself.

Ask Questions

Asking thought, opinion, and fantasy questions is a great way to banter and flirt with women. Approach and say, "Excuse me, I can't stay long, I have to get back to my friends, but I need to ask a question." Then ask a poll question, opinion question, fun question, information question, etc. When breaking into a group, pay attention to the person who is most responsive. Then, draw in other members of the group as well, especially the shy or quiet one. Some examples of questions to ask:

"I need someone to take a picture of me and friends, who is the best photographer?"

After one of them has taken your picture, show her the picture she has taken. Take a picture of her or the group and then show them the picture. Continue chatting with them if they seem to have high interest.

"My friends and I were having a discussion and we need an opinion: what would you think about a man in his mid-30s (or pick the age of the women) and has never been married? Would you consider that a red flag?"

"Who here knows the most about fashion? My friends tell me I need to update my look. I think I should start with my hairstyle, they think I should start with my clothes. What do you think?"

"I call you up and tell you that you have 30 minutes to pack your bikini and passport and you can pick our destination. Where are we going?"

The question above is one of my favorites, both in person and in text because it accomplishes several things:

- You are telling her what to do (both in the question and in the fantasy).
- You can see how she follows.
- You can see if she has an imagination.
- You can test for interest.

- You can use it to get to know her better. "Have you been there before? Where else have you been tropical?"
- The fantasy includes you and her together. By her responding, you have become bonded to her in her mind.
- You can find out if she is comfortable in her body (bikini) and if she is sensual.
- You can see if she is naturally spontaneous.

You can ask any question; it really doesn't matter. Don't just memorize questions and openers and run them mechanically. Ask questions or make statements that are interesting to you and reflect your personality. Use the answers as a way to continue the conversation if there is a high interest response.

Humor and Playfulness

Humor is a powerful tool for bantering and flirting, and it is almost impossible to banter and flirt without it. Studies have shown that people who use humor in social encounters are perceived as more likable. Humor also stimulates trust and attraction. Judicious use of humor can reduce anxiety and establish a relaxed mood.

Being humorous and playful isn't about telling jokes – it's about using the context of the situation in a novel or unexpected way. It can be as simple as stating, "Lovely day, isn't it?" during a torrential downpour. Here are some additional exchanges that work well for creating a sensual, playful context:

- *Alternate between being serious and silly.* Tell her you have to ask her a very personal and intimate question. Look very intense, lean forward, pause, then quietly ask her something very nonsensical, i.e., if she knows where the bathroom is or if she thinks Destiny's Child will ever get back together.
- *Pick something she has said and keep repeating it back to her in different, unrelated contexts.* "That's right, you're honest MOST OF THE TIME."
- *Tease her about something she has revealed about herself.* "Wow, you really are high maintenance!"

- *Tease her about a physical or verbal blunder she has made or something about what she is wearing that is out of place.* "I think leg warmers really are making a comeback!"
- *Tease her about where she is from, where she went to school, the music she listens to, or what sports team she likes.* "The Spice Girls, oh my God, I swear I won't tell a soul!" But of course, bring it up every chance you get and tell everyone who walks by.
- *Boast about yourself with a twinkle in your eye.* "I was the state debate champion in high school, want to argue with me?"
- *Flip her shit.* (To a barista in a coffee shop) "You've been making my drink every morning for a week and you can't even remember what I order! I must not mean much to you!"
- *Give her a nickname.* Pick something that sounds like her name or that is based on your conversation. Ask her if she had a nickname when she was a kid. Keep calling her by the nickname. If you call her later and ask her out, use her nickname. She'll remember you.

Teasing

Teasing creates anxiety for a lot of men. Many tell me that they were teased in hurtful and unloving ways as children. As adults, they are sensitive to being teased and tend to avoid teasing others. If this is true for you, you may have a difficult time distinguishing teasing that is mean and hurtful from teasing that is playful and loving. *When you tease a woman, always do it with a smile. Never be mean, critical, or demeaning.* Invite her in and open her up with your humor.

You can practice teasing with guy friends. This is a primary way that men express affection to each other. You can also *practice blurting.* As discussed above, this involves bypassing the editor in your mind and just saying what you are thinking. I've found that even really serious and boring guys often have funny, ironic or paradoxical thoughts that pop into their heads. Take a chance, let them out.

As paradoxical as it may sound, women respond with high interest when you tease them and bust on them. I conducted a poll of women and asked them why they are attracted to men who can make them laugh. Here are some of the responses I received:

- It relaxes them.
- It removes the fear of a possible agenda.
- It creates a feeling of security (like when she was a child and daddy tickled her or threw up into the air).
- It creates comfort.
- It makes her feel known.
- It releases anxiety.
- It implies intimacy and familiarity (you're not a stranger).
- It creates a bond.
- It implies strength and confidence.
- It implies flexibility and vulnerability.

Storytelling

Tell short stories about your life experiences that have a funny point, a paradox, embarrassing moment, unexpected outcome, or frustration. Always tell with humor and levity. Never be a victim (unless you can do it in a funny or self-depreciating way).

Most BDs have the tendency to talk too little or talk too much without observing whether or not anyone is even listening. For example, I was in my favorite restaurant a while back and a man and a woman in their 50's were sitting next to me. The woman was attractive and well dressed. The man was doing most of the talking and appeared to be very intelligent and well-traveled. It was obvious to me that they were having a glass of wine on a first date. The woman was attentive and leaning in toward the man. Her hands were on the table in the man's direction.

She would ask questions about the topic the man was talking about. The only problem was that the man talked almost non-stop about his life's travels. He gave way too much detail about mundane things and rarely paused. The only time he stopped talking, even momentarily, was when the woman leaned in and politely asked a question to show that she was listening. I wanted to shake the man and say, "This woman is a saint. She is attractive, classy, and attentive and you just keep droning on about some dull story. Stop. Take a breath. Ask her a question. Give her a chance to talk."

Learning to tell a story or share an opinion requires good conversation skills. *When you are talking, build and pause.* Ask the listener if she has had similar experiences. Make a statement that begs for more information and then stop. Make them ask the obvious question.

Eye contact is essential in conversation and storytelling. Once a conversation begins, it is normal to break eye contact as the speaker looks away. The person who is speaking frequently looks away more than the person who is listening. Turn-taking is governed by a characteristic pattern of looking, eye contact, and looking away. To signal that you have finished speaking and invite a response, look back at the other person again.

Interesting stories are never monologues. They don't drone on. They are an interactive process. Here's an example from my surfing experience in Sayulita, Mexico.

When I returned from a vacation to Mexico, people asked me how my trip was. I would say, "It was great, I had a great time." I smile and have open body language. This leaves it open for them to ask more questions.

"Where did you go? How was the weather?"

"I went to Puerto Vallarta for five days. The weather was spectacular, sunny and mid-eighties. Have you ever been to Puerto Vallarta?"

This invites them to join you in the experience, while creating a mood. You also find out about them.

I continue, "I spent two nights in a little fishing village called Sayulita."

Pause.

They ask, "Where is that?"

"It's about 30 miles north of Puerto Vallarta. It has a great beach for surfing, so I decided to take a surf lesson while I was there, it was a blast!"

They ask something like, "Did you get up on the surfboard? Did you wipe out?"

"Oh yeah, I wiped out every time! But a few times I actually stayed up for a few seconds and surfed! It was an amazing experience!"

This continues to set the mood. If you are flirting, you could make a sexual innuendo about the exhilaration of surfing and riding the wave.

I ask them, "Have you ever surfed?" Give them the chance to talk. You are guiding the conversation.

Add embarrassing moments. "I swallowed a lot of salt water! But all that salt water up my nose helped me get over a nagging sinus infection."

Add funny details, "My step-son was supposed to join me, but he couldn't get his passport in time."

"Really, that's too bad, how come? Did he wait too long to apply?"

"No, they wouldn't give him a passport because he has a warrant out on him." Pause for effect. "For urinating in public." Pause for effect. "Heaven knows they don't want to let any more people into Mexico who pee in public!" (This story is 100% true)

More Fun

In addition to asking questions, making statements, or telling stories, you can do physical things. Walk up to a woman and ask if she salsa dances. Whatever she says, approach her with your arms in a dance position. If she says "yes," say "good, I am taking lessons and I need to practice." Take her and start counting a salsa beat while you do a basic step and then spin her. If she doesn't salsa, say "I am taking lessons, let me show you a basic step."

Or, hold out your hand to a woman with your thumb up. Say, "I haven't done this in years." Take her hand and thumb wrestle.

Tell her to tell you her favorite dumb joke from when she was a kid. Tell her your favorite dumb childhood jokes.

Segue into telling her to tell you her favorite dirty joke. Have one of your own in mind (Q: "What are the three words you never want to hear when you are making love?" A: "Honey, I'm home!")

It's fun to propose contests, dares, and deals when bantering and flirting. Typical drinking contests fit in this category.

Make bets, dare the other person to do something, make deals – "If you do this, I'll do that."

Challenge her to a game of naming the state capitals. The loser has to buy the next round or do something embarrassing.

Play, "Fuck, Marry, Kill." Each of you gets to pick out three people in the room that the other person has to decide which they would fuck, marry, or kill.

Conclusion

After all is said and done, if you are having problems thinking of what to say to a woman, it is probably because she is showing low interest. So, move on. When a woman shows high interest, conversations are usually a breeze. Bantering and flirting will seem natural and spontaneous.

Resources

I would like to acknowledge the following resources for information used in this chapter:

IRC Guide to Flirting: http://www.sirc.org/publik/flirt.html

CHAPTER 18: FOLLOW THIS ROADMAP TO FIND YOUR REALLY GREAT WOMAN

How you date determines the kind of relationship you end up with.

When I was teaching the material in this book as online courses, most men registered for one of three reasons. Some wanted to improve their dating skills. Others wanted to find a friend with benefits (FWB). Most wanted to find love. If you fit in the third category, this chapter will completely change your paradigm about how to date.

The way most people date is absolutely the worst possible foundation upon which to build a healthy relationship. Here is how the average bad dater approaches dating:

- He has absolutely no plan and no idea what he is looking for. He just knows he is lonely and he believes a girlfriend is the answer to what ails him.
- If he is lucky, he meets a woman who shows some interest in him.
- If she isn't too unattractive (or too attractive, for that matter), he works up the nerve to ask her out.
- He does his best to make a good impression.
- If they seem to hit it off, he starts chatting with her on the phone and emailing on a daily basis.
- He sees her as often as he can and gives up most of the things that are important to him in order to be with her.

- If she is willing, they typically start having sex after just a few dates.
- He ignores all red flags and warning signs.
- Even if the relationship starts going south, he does everything he can to keep it together. He doesn't want to go back to being lonely, nor does he want to start the process of dating all over again.

Sound familiar? If you have been down this road before, you know where this approach leads – *getting stuck with a woman who disappoints you and/or drives you crazy.*

This chapter will show you how to greatly increase your odds of finding a Really Great Woman. This is the kind of woman who will bless your life, challenge you in healthy ways, and bring out the best in you. You might stumble onto a Really Great Woman when following the traditional model of dating. But let's not leave something this important to chance or dumb luck. This chapter contains a road map that will take you to your destination with the fewest detours and in the shortest amount of time.

The 5/5

The first order of business is to determine what you are looking for. As simple as this sounds, most BDs never write down the characteristics they want in a woman. This action is essential. If you don't know what you are looking for, you will probably never find it.

To find a Really Great Woman, you need an objective way of measuring and evaluating the women you date. You could be with a woman who is terribly wrong for you and not know it until it is way too late. Your quest for finding an RGW starts with your 5/5.

The 5/5 is a simple exercise. Write down at least five traits you *have to have* in a woman and five traits you *won't tolerate.* Five isn't a magic number in either category, but it is a good start. Start by drawing a line down the center of a piece of paper. Write "Have to Have" on the left side of the page and "Won't Tolerate" on the right side. Then start making your lists.

Have to Haves

A woman must have all of the traits on your "have to have" list to be your Really Great Woman. The traits on this part of your 5/5 will probably include things like honesty, fidelity, passion, sense of humor, availability, financial stability, and of course, passion and sex.

Won't Tolerate

The second part of the 5/5 is a list of things you won't accept in a woman or won't tolerate in a relationship. The *won't tolerates* are the deal killers. These might include deceit, infidelity, addictions, sloth, laziness, anger issues, mood disturbances, etc.

Sometimes the traits on each side of the page are just the opposite of the traits on the other side. That's okay. Observing these traits from two different sides will help you be clear on what you want and what you don't.

Your 5/5 list will reflect your personal wants and likes. Your list may evolve and grow over time. A good idea would be to post this list where you can see it regularly. Put it on your refrigerator or bathroom mirror. Review it often, especially when you start dating a new woman. I suggest that after three or four dates with a woman, you show her your 5/5 list and talk about what you are both looking for.

The Relationship Pyramid

The relationship pyramid is the second part of finding an RGW. Think of it as your guide for finding what you are looking for. It is a powerful tool for keeping you conscious. This diagram is a simple but elegant way to evaluate the women you date.

The Dating Essentials for Men Workbook (contained in the Dating Essentials for Men Bonus Bundle: https://datingessentialsformen.com/bonus-bundle) has a printable version of the relationship pyramid. You can draw one yourself on a blank piece of paper. Start by drawing a large pyramid. You will then draw three horizontal lines within the pyramid. The line closest to the bottom of the pyramid will take up about 20% of the pyramid space. The line closest to the top of the pyramid will take up less than 5% of the available space. This line should extend a little bit outside each side of the pyramid. The final line will be below this top line and will take up about 20% of the pyramid. You should now have four spaces in your pyramid. Label the spaces from top to bottom as follows: RGW, GW, WW, RWW.

Here are the basics of how the pyramid works: Every woman on the planet falls somewhere inside the pyramid. Every woman you meet will fall into a specific category when it comes to her suitability as a partner for you. Since every woman is measured from your personal perspective, the pyramid is subjective.

The dating pyramid helps you efficiently find a Really Great Woman by helping you quickly decide who is not a RGW. The pyramid ensures that you don't spend too much time with the wrong woman. Here are the four levels of the Pyramid:

Really Great Woman (RGW)

The upper tip of the pyramid is the *Really Great Woman*. An RGW is the only woman with whom you will enter into a long-term relationship. This is why there is a line extending out to either side of the pyramid. This line is to remind you that you don't go below that line when it comes to long-term relationships. This line reminds you to never settle or *date down.*

Your RGW is a woman with whom you could spend a lifetime. This woman meets every quality on your 5/5. *There is nothing fundamental about her that you would change.* You like her just as she is. This doesn't mean she is perfect, it just means there is nothing significant that you would ever want to change about her.

Don't confuse the idea of an RGW with *The One.* Don't fall into the trap of *oneitis.* I don't believe there is a one perfect woman for each man. Any number of women could be an RGW for you. Don't get caught up in the fantasy of looking for that one perfect woman who can complete you. Also, don't confuse the idea of an RGW with perfection, a *unicorn*, or a *key-holding goddess.*

Also, I warn against proclaiming a woman you have only known for three weeks to be your RGW. I believe it takes a good three years to truly know another person. I've listened to too many men breathlessly tell me they believe they've found their RGW after three dates, only to find out later that she can't commit or that she starts accusing him of infidelity if she sees him checking his cell phone or he shows up five minutes late for a date.

Good Woman (GW)

The *good woman* is just that, a good woman. I tell guys that there are "boatloads" of good women out there. Good women have many of the traits on your 5/5, but they don't score 100%. There may be one major thing from your 5/5 or an accumulation of smaller things that prevent them from being your RGW. The key difference between an RGW and a good woman is that *the GW has some fundamental things about her that you would want to change.*

If you get into a long-term relationship with a woman who has things about her you wish were different, two potentially negative things will probably happen. *The first is that you will constantly try to change her.* These attempts to get your GW to change will often be subtly manipulative. You might not always even be aware of it yourself. *Trying to change someone is unloving.* If you have ever been in a relationship with a woman who wanted you to be different in some fundamental way, you know what I mean.

The second potential problem with getting into a long-term relationship with a GW is that *you will always be at least a little dissatisfied with her.* This dissatisfaction may linger beneath the surface most of the time, but it will always be there. You will wish she was different. You might live with mild regret for settling. You'll fantasize about what it might be like to be with a woman who has the traits you desire. The cumulative effect is that you will become resentful, emotionally withdrawn, and ripe for an affair or some other form of sexual acting out (porn, chat rooms, etc.).

This is why you should never settle. Remember, *every time you settle, you end up with exactly what you settled for.* Don't fool yourself into thinking that a GW will either change over time or that you will come to accept her the way she is. This rarely happens and neither is being loving toward yourself or her. Never enter into a long-term relationship with any woman who doesn't have all the qualities on your list.

Wrong Women (WW)

Wrong women make up the majority of the women you will meet. These women are wrong for you for a number of reasons – age, language barriers, educational or economic differences, relationship status, etc. This isn't making a judgment about their character or person. WW are *wrong* because they are not a good match for you. Most women won't be, just like you won't be a good match for most women.

You are going to meet a lot of wrong women. You'll usually know it in 30 seconds or less. Sometimes, it might take a few minutes or a couple of hours to know for sure, but it usually doesn't take long. You'll typically be able to tell if a woman is wrong for you because you'll have little in common, you might not be attracted to her, or you might not be drawn to her personality. It goes without saying that you shouldn't waste time pursuing a relationship with a woman once you realize that she is wrong for you.

All women with whom you work are wrong women – never date them. There are too many things that can go wrong, from creating a messy work environment to you losing your job. All it takes is one woman (who seemed to be showing high interest) to tell your manager or HR that you are making her uncomfortable or harassing her. Best case scenario – you get a reprimand in your permanent file. Worst case scenario – you'll be looking for another job with a dark cloud hanging over you. No woman is worth this risk.

Really Wrong Women (RWW)

The bottom band of the relationship pyramid is reserved for *really wrong women*. This category consists of the women who will make your life miserable. RWW are disasters waiting to happen. Getting involved with one of these women may haunt you for the rest of your life. Steer a wide path around these women. Just so you'll know what we are talking about, here is a partial list of traits to be on the watch for (and avoid):

- Unavailable (*ghosts*)
- Dishonest, deceitful
- *Drama Queens*: Moody, insecure, jealous, or self-righteous
- Angry, rageful, abusive, resentful, passive-aggressive, or vindictive
- Controlling, demanding, or manipulative
- Critical, demeaning, argumentative (*gaslighters*)

- Perpetual victim and/or man-hater
- Borderline personality disorder (BPD), bi-polar, obsessive, or chronically depressed
- Unrecovered sexual abuse
- Obsessive need for male attention, history of infidelity
- Addiction: alcohol, drugs, spending, shopping
- Eating disorders (obesity, bulimia, anorexia)

You will recognize the average, run-of-the-mill WW quickly. Unfortunately, when BDs hook up with a RWW, they usually stay involved way too long. There are two reasons for this. The first is that *really wrong women are often very seductive.* They use their sexuality, their anger, their helplessness, their neediness, their humor and their intelligence to seduce.

The second reason is that *her dysfunction fits so well with your own.* I call this "Dysfunction X 2." You will be attracted to the worst kind of woman for you because she gives you the opportunity to play out your own dysfunction. If you have no boundaries, if you're acting out a need to rescue an unhappy woman (mother), or if it feels normal to be criticized, treated badly, or abandoned, a RWW will look really attractive to you – and she will eat you alive!

This is why the 5/5 is so important. Not only will it help you identify your RGW, it will also help you quickly spot RWW. Without your 5/5 to guide you, some RWW might actually look like your RGW. Some really wrong women may seemingly possess some of the traits you are look-ing for. Unfortunately, these traits typically aren't present the majority of the time, and they are often overshadowed by some really undesirable tendencies. At the first hint of unavailability, rage, jealousy, control, infi-delity, addiction, bitterness toward past partners, moodiness, argumen-tativeness – RUN! Don't look back!

How the Pyramid Works

The traditional dating process typically involves people putting their best foot forward in an attempt to be accepted by the person to whom they are attracted. Most people aren't their true selves. This doesn't necessarily mean that people are phony when they start dating, but pretty close to it. Both the man and the woman typically put a lot of energy into looking good, acting good, being attentive, being affectionate, and being sexual. Most folks try to demonstrate what a great catch they are.

This is why typical dating won't help you find an RGW. Everyone puts on a game face and tries their best to win the approval of the other. It isn't until somewhere down the line that both people start discovering who the other *really* is. By then, they are so enmeshed and so dependent on each other (and probably having sex regularly) that making corrections can be problematic.

In order to find a really great woman, you have to go as slowly as possible to find out as quickly as possible what her nature is (and how she fits into your life).

In addition, you have to know what you are looking for. The goal of pyramid dating is to discover a woman's nature as quickly as possible. By going slow you can get a clearer picture of her nature. At the same time, you can consult your 5/5 to see how she measures up.

Red & Yellow Flags

As you get to know a woman, you should be watching for red and yellow flags. Red flags are based on your 5/5. If, for example, a deal killer on your "Won't Tolerate" list is *addictions*, and a woman you are dating gets drunk every time you are with her, that's a red flag.

When you see a potential red flag, pay attention to it. This is one of the biggest mistakes BDs make – ignoring red flags, minimizing them, or thinking they will change. If your primary goal is to determine a woman's nature, these red flags are one of the most important details to which you need to pay attention. Don't rationalize away behaviors that don't fit your list. Finding your RGW requires that you be honest with yourself.

Yellow flags are little things that might not be on your 5/5, but which catch your attention as you get to know a woman. These are things you'll mentally note and keep an eye on in case they are an indicator of a bigger problem. Examples might be a woman's tendency to run late, not balance her checkbook, be rigid, be a little too involved with her kids, or keep old boyfriends hanging around as "friends."

As you observe a woman's nature, pay more attention to what she does than what she says. Her behavior defines her. This means that early in the dating cycle, you will be constantly testing, while observing what a woman does. Test for the items that are on your 5/5. Test for honesty, passion, flexibility, sense of humor, and sense of adventure.

A Numbers Game

The philosophy of the Relationship Pyramid is that finding a Really Great Woman is a numbers game. You have to meet and test a lot of women to find an RGW. The Pyramid helps you do this effectively.

A lot of men tell me that their biggest fear around dating is that they will get involved with the wrong kind of woman. I tell them that there is no way to avoid this. In order to find a princess, you have to kiss a lot of frogettes (or something like that). The dating pyramid allows you to meet a lot of good women and wrong women without getting caught up in an ongoing dysfunctional relationship. Out of this throng of women, an RGW can rise to the top.

Women who have the potential to be your RGW make up only a small fraction of the total number of women out there. They are few and far between. This is why it is essential that you know what you are looking for – so that you can walk through the open door when it presents itself.

After you meet a woman, go as slowly as possible to find out as quickly as possible what her nature is. Follow the rules. Keep checking your 5/5. Practice being a good ender (Chapter 19). You have the roadmap and directions; the rest is up to you.

CHAPTER 19: PRACTICE THE MOST IMPORTANT DATING SKILL OF ALL – BE A GOOD ENDER

Being a good ender covers a multitude of dating sins.

W hen I got out of my second marriage in 2002, I faced a sober reality. I had been married to two women for a combined 25 years. Unfortunately, I shouldn't have gone out with either woman more than three times. Both women had good traits, but neither were close to being my Really Great Woman. So, when I became single in my 40s, I concluded that I needed to develop some new dating skills. But more than this, if I wanted to find an RGW, *I had to become a better picker AND a better ender.*

As I stated in the previous chapter – dating is a numbers game. You are going to meet some good women. You are going to meet a lot of wrong women. You are going to meet a few really wrong women. Since your goal is to only stay in a long-term relationship with a person who has the potential to be a Really Great Woman for you, *you have to learn how to recognize the women who aren't potential RGWs and break up quickly.*

Since you are going to meet a lot of women who won't qualify as really great for you, you need to successfully practice *catch and release* with these women. Otherwise, you will be in deep trouble. Being a good ender is essential to limiting the amount of time you spend with women who aren't potential RGWs while leaving the door open for meeting women who might be. Beyond this, *you can get away with being a bad picker if you are a good ender.* Being a good ender is the best dating insurance you can buy.

When I ask guys in my dating programs what their greatest fears are, "breaking up" is always in the top three. BDs tend to fear breaking up for a number of reasons:

- They are afraid it might be a mistake – they might regret it later.
- They might be seen as a "jerk."
- They don't want to hurt anyone.
- They fear a backlash from a negative societal view of men who dump women.
- As men, they are biologically and socially programmed to provide and protect.
- They fear a blow-up and/or reprisal.
- They have too much to lose.
- There might be kids involved.
- They hope it will get better.
- They have religious issues – "I made a commitment."

Even though it can be frightening to think about breaking up with a woman, it is an essential skill for finding the kind of woman who is worth spending a potentially large chunk of your life with.

Catch & Release

Here are the basics for breaking up effectively:

After one date: If you don't want to see her again after the first date, just shake her hand and say "It was nice to meet you. Good luck with your dating." This is code for "I'm not going to call you back." If she says she wants to see you again, tell her then that you don't feel enough chemistry to keep dating. Don't tell her you will call if you're not going to.

After two to three dates: If you have been on two or three dates and haven't had sex, it is okay to just quit calling. Or, you can send her an email telling her that you enjoyed getting to know her but don't feel enough chemistry to keep dating.

After a month or more (or regular sex): If you have been on several dates and/or are having sex, I suggest the following:

- Sooner is always better than later. It doesn't get easier after two weeks, two months, two years, or two kids. It only gets harder the longer you wait.
- Keep it short and to the point. Use the *Two Sentence Rule* ("Whatever needs to be said can be said best in two sentences or less").
- Never use the "It's not you, it's me" routine – It is bullshit. You are breaking up with her for one reason and one reason only: You have low interest in continuing to date her because she does not have the qualities to be your Really Great Woman.
- Don't try and give her a "reasonable" explanation. You are breaking up because you have *low interest*. It is that simple. Even if you used to have *high* interest, you don't have to explain what changed.
- Don't give her anything with which to argue or get you off the subject.
- Use "I" messages. "I am ending this..." Not, "We should end this..."
- Make a direct, powerful statement. Don't be wishy washy or use wishy washy words. "I need to end this...." not, "Maybe we should break up... "
- Don't try and soften it.
- Don't try and break it to her easy – she'll see it coming and have her defenses up.

Bad Breakup Strategies

Don't wait for a *Greyhound Divorce*. It is amazing how often I hear men who are in bad relationships (or in relationships with a woman who isn't an RGW) express a passive and unloving wish about their partner:

- I wish she would just leave me for another guy, then I won't have to break up with her.

- Maybe she'll get cancer and die and then I won't look like a schmuck for breaking up with her.
- Maybe she'll get hit by a Greyhound bus, so I don't have to end it.

A second common passive-aggressive approach to ending a relationship is to either be so unavailable for so long or to act so badly (cheat on her with her best friend, spend countless hours looking at online porn) that she finally gets fed up and kicks your ass out.

I call this destructive approach to breaking up the *Ben Affleck, Break up by Stripper* strategy. This label is a combination of the term "Suicide by Cop" (where a guy is too chicken-shit to kill himself, so he incites a cop to shoot him in self-defense) and actor Ben Affleck's way of getting J-Lo to dump him when she found out he was hanging out with strippers and dropping hundreds of thousands of dollars gambling in Vegas. (Considering that people like Affleck are followed by hordes of picture-snapping paparazzi, did he really think Jennifer wouldn't find out about his bad behavior?)

Breaking up is just one more facet of setting the tone in a relationship. If a woman is not your RGW, ending it is the loving and manly thing to do. Don't put it off or wait for it to die a slow, agonizing, dehumanizing death.

Better Breakup Strategies

As I have stated, women are security-seeking creatures. Therefore, a breakup will probably mess with a woman's sense of emotional (and perhaps financial) security. When you break up with a woman you have been dating, she might have a strong emotional reaction. That's okay. It doesn't mean you have done anything wrong.

You have to be willing to be seen as the "Jerk." Don't be a jerk, but allow her to project this on you so she can emotionally disengage from you. Keep in mind, she will probably bounce back quickly and be in a new relationship before you.

Here is one of the most important truths of successful dating: *You probably won't risk getting in if you are not sure you can get out.*

This is why learning to be a good ender is so essential to successful dating – both in terms of having the courage to initiate and having the courage to break up with a woman who isn't your RGW. If you know you can get out, you can date several women and risk getting *all in* with the women who look promising. And you can do so without the fear of being trapped and smothered.

If you follow the principles presented in this book, your break-ups should be pretty clean because you have been following the rules – going slow, testing, observing her nature, watching for red flags, and testing interest level (yours and hers).

Most break-ups get ugly because the guy waits way too long. You can break up lovingly and without drama if you follow the rules and do it as soon as you realize the woman isn't your RGW. I am still on very good terms with some ex-girlfriends because of the way I broke up with them. I did it in a timely manner, directly, and with love. As a result, these women still see me as a good man and stay in contact with me. That's not necessarily true for my ex-wives with whom I did not end things so well!

One of the things that helped some of the good breakups go as well as they did is that I had previously had what I call a *pre-breakup discussion* with these women. You might have this discussion along with the *pre-sex talk* or the *what are we* discussion. These are good times to talk about how you will break up. Odds are you will, so why not be mature and discuss how you will go about it.

Rather than fighting a lot, cheating, or pulling away from each other when it is time to break up, sit down and talk about it in the way you determined you would in your pre-breakup discussion. This allows both of you to get all the way in. Plus, it avoids unnecessary speculation, especially if the person thinking about breaking up seems a little distant or preoccupied from time to time.

I have had pre-breakup discussions with a few women I was starting to get serious with and they all appreciated it. I told them that they won't have to guess if I am losing interest – that I will sit down and talk with them about how I am feeling. This made the women feel safe about letting go and getting more deeply involved with me. When we did break up, we just followed the plan we had previously set up.

It doesn't matter if you are looking for love and a long-term relationship, or a short-term sexual encounter, being a good ender helps ensure that all of your experiences end as good as they began. Remember: Being a good ender can cover a multitude of sins when you make the occasional bad choice in a woman. Not only does it help you close the doors that need closing, but it will also help open new doors down the road.

DATING ESSENTIALS FOR MEN WRAP-UP

It works if you work it.

Conscious dating is a powerful, personal-growth machine. Not only will the principles in this book help you meet a lot of great women and get you laid, they will grow you as a man.

Conscious dating challenges you, gets you out of your comfort zone, teaches you new social skills, helps you face your fears and soothe yourself, and provides a roadmap for becoming a more powerful, integrated man.

Women are attracted to a man who looks like he knows where he is going and is having a good time going there.

The skills I teach in *Dating Essentials for Men* have resulted directly from my own dating experience. As I practiced the principles I have taught you, I met a lot of amazing women, had a lot of great sex, and enjoyed a handful of enriching long-term relationships.

Even more, from practicing the skills I teach in *Dating Essentials for Men*, my life has taken off in many other ways. My business is doing great, I live in Mexico, I do what I love, I am in good shape and good health, I have more than enough money, I wake up every day excited about the adventure, and I continuously encounter doors of opportunity that open in front of me.

Contrast this to where I was when I started dating in my late 40's. I was devastated from a divorce, overcoming a bankruptcy, not sure if my business was going to survive, struggling with depression and loneliness, and unsure of where my life was taking me.

What changed? It really was as simple as this:

- I got out of the house.
- I expanded my route.
- I talked to people everywhere I went.
- I tested for interest.
- I walked through open doors.
- I had fun.

My final words of advice to you:

- Keep working at it.
- Be gentle with yourself.
- Let go of attachment to outcome.
- Remember, it's all practice.

DR. ROBERT GLOVER

D r. Glover is the author of the groundbreaking book *No More Mr. Nice Guy.*

His website drglover.com features numerous online self-help courses, workshops, podcasts, groups, and trained coaches and therapists.

Contact Dr. Glover at: robert@drglover.com

MORE DATING ESSENTIALS FOR MEN RESOURCES

A s the creator of *Dating Essentials for Men*, Dr. Glover has empowered thousands of men to transform their lives. By helping them overcome self-limiting beliefs and learn effective dating skills, these men have become more social, found love and fulfilling relationships, and created satisfying sex lives.

Check out all of Dr. Glover's resources for single men at datingessentialsformen.com.

PLEASE LEAVE A REVIEW AND SPREAD THE WORD

Thank you for reading Dating Essentials for Men. For most books, sales are driven by word-of-mouth recommendations, online shares, and positive reviews. If you think other men will benefit from Dating Essentials for Men, please spread the word with friends and acquaintances, post your experience on social media and online forums, and leave a positive review on Amazon.com. Nothing helps an author more.

Made in United States
Troutdale, OR
11/09/2023

14432362R00116